How to Sell Well

SOME OTHER BOOKS BY JAMES F. BENDER

How to Sell Well

THE ART AND SCIENCE OF PROFESSIONAL SALESMANSHIP

James F. Bender

Sales Training and Marketing Consultant

McGRAW-HILL BOOK COMPANY, INC.

New York   Toronto   London

Memo .

To: The Reader
From: The Author
About: The Approach

A few years ago the Board of Trustees of Yale University were looking for a president for their alma mater. A distinguished alumnus, Wilmarth S. Lewis, suggested a job specification:

"Yale's next president must first of all be a Yale man and a great scholar," Lewis said, "also a social philosopher who has at his finger tips the solution to all the world's problems from Formosa to birth control. He must be a good public relations man and an experienced fund raiser. He must be a magnificent speaker and a great writer. He must be a man of the world, yet he must also have great spiritual qualities—a great administrator who can delegate authority.

"He must be a leader, not too far to the right, nor too far to the left, and of course, not too much in the middle. He must be a man of iron health and stamina; a young man but also mature and full of wisdom. . . .

"As I have been talking, you have no doubt realized there is only one who has most of these qualifications. But there is a question, even about him. 'Is God a Yale Man?' "

The standards, pleasantly irreverent, were, you'll agree, impossibly high. Yet, I suspect, Yale found an excellent president simply because the standards were high.

Until just recently, the world of business—from Egypt's heyday on—never applied enough high standards. Traditionally, business expected us to blink at sharp practices and its ineptitudes. It was only yesterday that everyone accepted *caveat emptor*—let the buyer beware!

But a new day is upon us. American and Canadian big business is trying more conscientiously than has ever been tried before to promote high standards—standards of service, of products, of selecting employees to mind the standards. To all but the uninformed, the evidence is clear: the great majority of our business leaders are idealists—men and women who see the best way to succeed is to make ideals work on the job. Even if we can't always reach them, they say, we need ideals to use, to stretch, to multiply our potentialities.

Modern salesmanship is a case in point. American and Canadian business leaders are imposing the highest standards upon their salesmen. Contrast the sales representative of the 1960s with his typical forebears. You find him better educated and trained. He's aware of his responsibilities as a high-level businessman. By standards of motivation, study, conduct, and service he deserves the professional status he's winning.

Because of his training, the professional salesman considers the objection raised by critics of salesmanship (and advertising)—that the use of motivation is wrong because it permits him to manipulate customers and buyers against their will—a false premise. His answer, full of common sense and conviction, is: customers never realized the benefits of central heating, life insurance, vacuum cleaners, deodorants, antibiotics, toilet tissue, sanitary protection, toothbrushes until salesmanship created (or educated) a desire for such items. His answer is full of ethics, too. For he won't sell shoddy products or questionable services. Neither will he persuade customers to buy beyond their capacity to use what he sells. As a professional salesman, he considers himself an educator and servant of mankind—a proponent of the enterprise system.

It is to him that this book is addressed—to the man dedicated to salesmanship as a career and a profession. That is, direct salesmanship in which the salesman calls on buyers. The book takes the salesman (or prospective salesman) through the basic steps of entering into and succeeding in salesmanship.

Most of the chapters deal with basic principles and applications that other kinds of salesmen—for example, retail, door-to-door—can also use. Much of the illustrative matter applies to salesmen who work for large companies. However, smaller companies and salesmen working for themselves can and often do follow the same procedures and strive for similar goals.

The book has three parts: the salesman (or prospective salesman) is introduced to (1) the current standards of salesmanship and the steps to take to find a company to work for and to be hired by; (2) the basic things to do to sell more effectively; (3) a plan and exercises for self-study. It involves him in high standards and worthy ideals; it advises him how to work hard and efficiently and to conduct himself admirably. The seasoned salesman may also use the book—to review his skills and attitudes.

The book can be used in other ways too. The sales manager, looking for materials to use in sales meetings with his salesmen, will find it an instruction manual. It can be used, as indeed most of the materials in it have been used, as a text for salesmen in training programs. It includes material for group discussions and class exercises. You see, I have tried to make it a practical book.

Some of the ideas in it were discussed in my course for salesmen and sales managers—over a period of eight years—at Columbia University's Institute of Arts and Sciences, and more recently at C. W. Post College of Long Island University. Many of the ideas grew out of the stimulating contacts I had teaching salesmen and executives—for over eighteen years—of organizations such as: Bigelow-Sanford Carpet Co.; Central Hudson Gas & Electric Co.; Financial Public Relations Association; Foote, Cone & Belding, Hennis Freight Lines; International Cellucotton Products Co.; International Business Machines Corporation; Johns-Manville Corporation; Johnson & Johnson (Ortho-Pharmaceutical and Ethicon Medical Products Divisions); Kimberly-Clark Corporation; Lehigh Coal & Navigation Co.; Lever Bros. Co.; Meadow Brook National Bank; National Bakery Division of A & P Food Stores; Service Bureau Corporation; Standard Financial Corporation; The Welsbach Corporation.

I have tried to write in simple, conversational style—so that the casual reader can skim the book. However, to get the most from it, the salesman or sales executive should study it, chapter by chapter, and should do the occasional assignments.

My gratitude springs from many sources. I am particularly indebted to the salesmen and executives with whom

I have worked. For it was they who helped me run the winnowing machine. The late A. R. Hahn, editor of *Sales Management*, extended helpful suggestions on a number of the chapters when I wrote them as articles for that excellent magazine.

Mrs. D. A. Dustman was most helpful in typing much of the manuscript. Most of all, I am indebted to my wife, Anne Parsons Bender, for her patience, inspiration, and editorial acumen. I wish to thank Mrs. E. Lefevre, widow of the author of *Reminiscences of a Stock Operator* for permission to quote from that interesting book.

If we in the U.S.A. and Canada are to continue to succeed as champions of free opportunity, we shall need more well-trained salesmen; salesmen who think of their vocation in terms of professional status.

May this book serve, however modestly, those worthy ends.

James F. Bender
C.W. Post College
Brookville, L.I., New York

Contents

PART 1

Getting the Right Job

1

The Growing Profession of Salesmanship

> The true worth of a man is to be measured by the work he pursues.
>
> AURELIUS

As a human being, you're the most adaptable inhabitant of the animal kingdom. That's why salesmanship is only one of many vocations in which you can excel. For you carry in you the capacities to succeed—to a greater or lesser extent—in at least 10,000 vocations. *Dictionary of Occupational Titles* lists more than 20,000!

In Julius Caesar's day, thousands of potential airplane pilots went to Rome. But they worked at other jobs, simply because airplanes weren't invented. As it was then, so is it now. Just last year the U.S. Labor Department had to add 375 brand-new occupations to its *Dictionary of Occupational Titles.* Ten years hence, our children will adapt themselves to many vocations now unknown. The comforting thought is: Man always meets the challenge of new careers—of the changing complexities of vocations. His vast adaptability ever ensures great success.

3

Some vocations, such as horseshoer, peter out. Others—baker, for instance—were popular in early Egypt and are still going strong. They thrive in all civilizations. Still other vocations begin humbly; grow in importance; become professions. An example is the surgeon. Three hundred years ago the barber doubled as surgeon.

Anatomy of a profession

What does a vocation need to become a profession? First, a body of knowledge and theory complex enough to require systematic study. Second, deep devotion to the ideal of service. Third, loyalty to the chosen profession—to help make it better. Fourth—and most basic—gifted people to serve it.

As the resourceful surgeon's practice grew, he gave up barbering. He specialized. He sought courses at the university in anatomy and other subjects. He discussed with doctors (teachers) and classmates theories and techniques. These he found in textbooks and lecture halls. Later he worked under supervision in clinics and laboratories.

His devotion to his studies, to the service of mankind, demanded great sacrifices on his part—both as student and later as practitioner. He couldn't close up shop at sundown or go on strike. He was on call twenty-four hours a day—to alleviate human suffering. He didn't charge by the hour—a sum set by a guild or union. He tempered his fee to the patient's ability to pay.

To enter his profession he had to win a license or degree. He had to pass examinations, carefully prepared, administered, and scored by faculties. To maintain his standing in his profession, he had to continue to study after he began to practice. From time to time he would return to university or clinic to take a refresher course. Sometimes he would seek out a famous colleague to learn a new technique from him. Between times, he read his journals of surgery and medicine—always in search of new ideas and skills to increase his proficiency.

He still continues to do these things today. And more too. He participates in the activities of his professional organizations, such as The American College of Surgeons or American Medical Association. He attends their conventions; conducts demonstration clinics; shares his discoveries through the articles and books he writes. Like Chaucer's Clerk of Oxford, gladly does he learn and gladly teach. As an alumnus he's deeply concerned about the welfare of his alma mater. He wants to help keep it abreast, if not ahead, of other distinguished colleges and universities.

Salesmanship: vocation or profession?

Let's recall how far and fast salesmanship has come in just a few years. If you were a manufacturer—in America's and Canada's pioneer days—you worked at home. If you made more of your product than your family (and neighbors) used, you sold your surplus to a peddler. The peddler carried his pack (or pushed his cart) and knocked on doors. The housewife came out to see his wares—pie pans, thimbles, whale-oil lamps, and the like.

From peddler to drummer to salesman

The peddler developed into a "drummer." As the railroads crisscrossed the continent, drummers rode them. They carried news, stories, and especially new products. Some were unscrupulous men who never made call-backs. They wouldn't dare to. Most of them were honorable men who built regular routes—sometimes fortunes—on sound merchandise, faithful service. They were the messengers and providers of the ever-higher standard of living, so precious to Americans and Canadians.

A hundred years ago, manufacturers—such as Pattison Bros. of tinware fame—substituted their own specialty salesmen for drummers. Pattison Bros. was perhaps the first firm to set regular territories and routes for their salesmen. This spread. It resulted in brand names and other developments.

According to the late Merle Thorpe, New England axes were the first to have their own names. Manufacturers stamped packing cases with hot irons. That's how "brands" became household words. "Remington," "Winchester," "Colt" were among the early ones. Ever since, a brand name has been protection for the buyer and a salesman's best friend.

Not until 1870 did the Census Bureau recognize salesmen as belonging to a specialized vocation. "Commercial travelers" the census named them. There were 7,000 of them in that year!

At about this time, the "traveler"—he's still often called that in Canada—established jobbers and distributors. He practiced the laying on of hands to increase distribution and its benefits. In this decade also, our first advertising agencies came into being. Advertising was established in those days as printed salesmanship.

Later in the century, John H. Patterson of National Cash Register Co. pioneered a training course for his salesmen. In the same era, The Wharton School at University of Pennsylvania was established. Here subjects related to salesmanship were taught. Early in the present century, the Harvard Business School came into being—to promote graduate study in business, marketing, and kindred subjects.

During the early days of the Great Depression, National Sales Executives, Inc., was founded. Subsequently, NSE sponsored—as it does today—courses of study at leading universities for salesmen and sales executives.

The growing climate of professionalism

Company training programs for salesmen continue to expand. Many of these cover more than just product information and coaching in direct selling. Some of them include the concept of "personal progress." They provide —in addition to indoctrination and on-the-job training— each salesman with an individualized program of personal development. Based on regular performance reviews, the salesman's development program is geared to his changing needs.

Kimberly-Clark Corporation, for example, recently established its institute of marketing. Here K-C gives training programs—at several levels—to its salesmen and other members of its marketing division. Newly hired salesmen spend two weeks at the institute. They study principles of marketing, creative merchandising, business writing and speaking, sales promotion techniques, etc. They spend 120 hours in classes, conferences, study hall, and interviews in the two weeks! They must pass examinations to win a diploma. Kimberly-Clark also provides advanced programs in the institute for seasoned salesmen and marketing executives.

Service Bureau Corporation, subsidiary of IBM, holds a five-week school for its newly inducted salesmen. NCR also regards selling as a science that calls for intensive training, for a detailed knowledge of the customer and his requirements. A saying is: "An NCR salesman never graduates." The statement isn't an exaggeration. NCR salesmen

—as indeed those of many other of our leading companies —start studying the day they're hired. They don't finish until the day they leave.

Some life insurance companies send their salesmen to a 22-week training course at universities. Such a course is carefully planned by company executives in collaboration with university faculties. After graduation the salesmen continue to periodically take both in-company and on-campus refresher courses.

You could mention hundreds of other examples—of companies investing huge sums in the education of their salesmen. Their experience indicates that salesmen are made, not born.

Salesmen aren't born

Young men sometimes select selling as a career because they are "born salesmen." Training-minded companies don't support that theory. They're always eager, of course, to find men with natural gifts in that direction. But they've learned that a successful salesman needs something more than an engaging smile, a sales kit, and stout shoe leather. They don't accept Georgie Gobel's definition "A salesman is a fella with a smile on his face, a shine on his shoes, and a lousy territory."

More and more the accent is on the attitudes and skills derived from study and training—skills aimed at analyzing the customers' needs and supplying them intelligently. This means grueling hours of study and learning—of sys·tems, product information, territory analysis, the psychology of empathy, time management, and the like. The pleasing personality is taken for granted. That is, the applicant must demonstrate initially—by appearance, speech, and manners—that he's of professional caliber. Only then will they invest in him a sustained program to prepare him for a career of service and self-improvement.

To be worthy of the title "Professional Salesman," he must be imbued with the ideal of service. His accent is on helping people to buy intelligently rather than "loading them up." He's keenly aware of his responsibilities and contributions to the free enterprise system. If he were to fail in bolstering a dynamic economy, our basic freedoms might be no more. He knows this. He's intelligent enough to appreciate that the kind of service he extends has effects— far beyond those reflected in his take-home pay.

Like the surgeon, the modern salesman has his basic training, his professional organization, his refresher courses, his specialized reading and study—to keep him abreast of the best that is thought and said in sales psychology, merchandising, market and consumer research, and allied subjects. The day is perhaps not far off when the salesman, like the surgeon, will be licensed—as indeed is already the case with salesmen of life insurance and investments in some countries and states.

Benefits of training the professional salesman

The list of companies—both small and large—expanding their training programs grows daily. They find that training and education of their salesmen—and others— results in benefits. Among those they most often emphasize are:

1. Increased sales and profits
2. More satisfied customers
3. Lower turnover among their salesmen
4. Development of their salesmen for positions of increasing responsibility within the company
5. More job satisfaction for their salesmen

6. Improved teamwork and higher morale
7. Greater status for the position of salesmen
8. More prestige for salesmen in the eyes of their families and friends—more cooperation from the salesmen's wives

With all these developments—in colleges and universities, in progressive companies, among professional organizations—the modern salesman is provided a climate of professionalism. The farsighted salesman, therefore, looks upon his responsibilities in a mature way. He's a high-level businessman who considers salesmanship a profession. His success depends upon his capacities, his training and study, his attitudes, the kind of company he joins.

Let's sketch, next, the profile of the professional salesman.

2

Marks of the Professional Salesman

> Help your profession to grow in influence by good deeds.
>
> HARRY IRELAND

Sizes of success

Successful salesmen come in all sizes and shapes. A life insurance company reports that its top salesman—three years in a row—is 5 feet 3 inches tall, weighs 125 pounds. Another life insurance company's leading salesman stands 6 feet 6 inches and treads the scales at 275 pounds.

A paper company—having 500 salesmen—selects its 10 best salesmen of consumer products each year. They join the "Winner's Circle" because of their outstanding success. As you'd suppose, these 10 winners don't conform to a physical type. They're short and tall, fat and lean, long- and round-headed, bald and thatched, light and dark, old and young. They're themselves. But they're themselves at their best.

Psychologists have never found any meaningful correlation between success in selling and physical traits. In other words, there's no such thing as a salesman-type. There are

only individual salesmen. This means success in salesmanship depends upon other factors. And we shall discuss these
throughout the book.

Some facts and figures

Despite our dependence on salesmen for our economic
well-being, we have too few statistics about them. *The
American Salesman* recently did a study for its readers to
supply them with some facts about salesmen. *The American Salesman,* edited at 355 Lexington Avenue, New York
City, engaged the professional research firm of Erdos &
Morgan to supervise the study.

They sent out a questionnaire to 2,000 salesmen, sub-
scribers to *The American Salesman;* received replies from
60 per cent- –without any follow-up! Among the interesting facts reported are these:

1. *Age:* Slightly under 40 years, the median.
2. *Travel:* Eighty-two per cent travel, 13 weeks away from
   home is the median figure. 14 per cent have to spend 30
   or more weeks a year away from home. Nearly half of
   them have company cars. The median mileage they cover
   in company cars is 22,670 a year. The slightly larger
   group drives a median distance of 17,614 miles a year on
   sales calls—in their own cars.
3. *Income:* The range of income is from $5,000 (2 per cent)
   a year to more than $20,000 (10 per cent). The median
   for the group was $10,604. This latter figure is said to be
   greater by $2,000 than the median income for lawyers.
4. *Investments:* Two-thirds reported investment of part of
   their earnings. Nearly half of these have stocks. 14 per
   cent buy government bonds; the others reported investments in real estate, mutual funds, etc. Median life insurance coverage was $31,042.
5. *Home ownership:* Seventy-eight per cent own their own

homes. This compares with the national average of 60 per cent.

6. *Family status:* Ninety-three per cent are married. They have an average of 1.7 children (the same as Harvard graduates).

7. *Telephoning:* Median number of phone toll calls they make each month is 21, and one-sixth of the salesmen average 50 or more.

8. *Education:* Seventy per cent attended college. Comparable figure for the general population is 18 per cent.

9. *Training:* Thirty-six per cent received some formal training in salesmanship or marketing; 81 per cent found this training valuable.

10. *Reading:* Forty-seven per cent read 10 or more books a year besides several weekly and monthly periodicals.

Admittedly, these facts represent a small number of the nation's more than 4 million salesmen. But we can assume that this group represents the higher echelons of salesmen —those interested in improving their status. They qualify as a professionally minded group. The composite picture describes a serious, hard-working, substantial citizen—a far cry from the stereotyped salesman of stories.

Profiles of two kinds of salesmen

Over the past ten years psychologists, personnel specialists, and management engineers have made great strides in selecting salesmen. These experts use standardized tests, depth interviews, background studies to reach their conclusions. Then they share their findings with one another through their professional organizations and publications. Result: They make use of latest discoveries, and they don't rely on guessing.

For example, Eugene J. Benge, management engineer, tested 564 salesmen in a varied group of industries. He found 10 attributes that separated the high producers from those whose sales were unsatisfactory. You can use Benge's results—as he reported them in *Sales Management*—to etch the group profiles of successful and poor salesmen.

Attributes	Excellent men scored	Poor men scored	Per cent by which excellent men exceeded poor men
1. Self-confidence	84	48	75
2. Planning ability	82	47	74
3. Industriousness	83	52	60
4. Persuasiveness	85	56	57
5. Intelligence	77	52	48
6. Technical knowledge	79	55	44
7. Interest	89	62	44
8. Ambition	77	56	38
9. Health	83	64	30
10. Social development	82	65	26
Average score all 10 factors	82.1	55.6	48

Such studies give us insights into how groups of excellent and poor salesmen differ. They indicate the good group is about twice as able as the poor group but they tell us little about the individual, his job quandaries, how he goes about solving them successfully. Moreover, they don't clearly tell us where, for example, interest leaves off and ambition begins; or how the two mix.

Psychologists find almost 18,000 trait names in unabridged dictionaries—words that describe the personality, such as neatness, enthusiasm, honesty, sincerity. It's impossible to build a profile upon all of them to serve as a pattern of the top salesman. Life and the multiplicity of personality traits are too complicated for that. Perhaps a more useful tack for our purposes is to report four case studies of high-level salesmen. Then draw a general conclusion from them for salesmen to refer to, each using his own individuality for comparison.

The case of Eric Johnston

Eric Johnston, returning home to the Northwest after World War I, took a job selling vacuum cleaners. The first two weeks he didn't sell a single vacuum cleaner. But he kept on ringing doorbells every day. He reports that he wasn't discouraged; that each turndown *increased his interest* to find the right approach to sell cleaners. He worked long hours every day. By the third week he had perfected his skills and began to close sales. Before long he was the star salesman on the force. Notice: He trained himself.

A few years after, he became president of his company. Later he was chosen president of the Chamber of Commerce of the United States. At present he's head of the organization that represents Hollywood's motion picture industry. He says his basic interest remains in salesmanship; that each position he's ever held has been basically a salesman's challenge.

The case of Sidney Moser

At the age of sixty-eight, Moser was retired from the YMCA, where he had been a secretary most of his life. His wife became ill, and he had to supplement his pension. What was a man of sixty-eight to do? He answered an advertisement for salesmen of mutual investment shares. Moser took the company training course and sold on commission.

For the first six months his earnings averaged $10 a week. He says he was often discouraged but resolved to keep on trying. He could think of no other work open to him. He reports he worked faithfully full days and three evenings a week. Most of his contacts in the beginning were "leads" provided by the office.

As he analyzed his failure, he concluded he must specialize. The idea occurred to him to sell mutual shares to pension funds of small businesses. He arbitrarily selected businesses with fewer than 10 employees. He foresaw that once he sold the plan, the pension funds would be regular customers—adding to their holdings monthly.

This meant he had to tailor his sales presentation accordingly. Before he approached the head of a small business, he gathered a lot of information about it. With this, he prepared a brochure of specific suggestions for each company head—used it in his initial presentation.

At the end of the first year of his specialized selling—when he was almost seventy years of age—his earnings were averaging $2,000 a month. "More money," he said, "than they've got at Fort Knox!"

The case of Rex Stout

If you like whodunits you may have read some of Rex Stout's. As a young man, Rex wrote bushels of blood-curdling yarns. He kept busy at them until 1916. In that year he became dissatisfied. He didn't like the size of the checks he got for his stories. And he wasn't happy with the quality of his work.

In his daydreams, Rex Stout said to himself, "If I had a business that would let me save $200,000 ... I could live off the income.... Then I'd have more time to do better writing ... could turn out novels I'd be proud of. ..." He continued to think about this idea—pulled it out of the clouds, grappled with it. As he cross-examined himself, he wrote down:

Q: What's the best way to make money?
A: Selling things.
Q: Who are the best people to sell things to?
A: People who always have money.
Q: What people always have money?

A: Bankers.

Q: What things can you sell to bankers?

At this point, Stout didn't have an answer. After wrestling with the problem for some time, he got an idea: What's the one thing bankers always need? Depositors!

Then came another stream:

Q: How can I deliver bankers a big block of depositors?

A: Almost everyone over twenty-one is already a depositor.

Q: What's wrong with people under twenty-one?

Now he hit pay dirt: "I'll sell them child depositors!"

Once he set his target, the rest was merely hard work. He called on public school superintendents all over the state. He arranged with bankers in each community to collect children's savings on Monday mornings. Pennies, nickels, dimes, and quarters rolled in. The schools and banks—working together through Stout's service—taught children to save money, to become thrift-conscious. He sold his service country-wide.

Rex Stout saved $400,000 in only eleven years! From then on he devoted the rest of his life to leisurely writing and public service.

The case of Thomas Bryce

His uncle financed Tom Bryce's education at an engineering college. Tom just squeaked through his studies to graduate. His uncle also helped him find a position with a steel company. He joined the sales department among other engineer-salesmen. He devoted six months to a sales training course provided by his company. Assigned to sell bridges, Bryce did pedestrian work until he became engaged to a girl of wealthy family.

After that, his work was marked by enthusiasm and creative ideas. For example, he suggested prefabricated

culverts to sell in rural areas. These became a very successful item. Bryce sold more of them than any of the other
salesmen. Within two years he became head of a subsidiary sales organization and married the girl.

Interest, industriousness, success marked the selling of
Eric Johnston, Sidney Moser, Rex Stout, Tom Bryce. But
notice the different incentives that sparked their success.

Evidently, Johnston plugged away because he liked the
challenge of salesmanship. Moser was at his wit's end. He
had to succeed to meet his bills. Stout's ulterior motive
(time to write leisurely) was strong enough to promote
years of intensive, intelligent selling. Through success in
sales, he foresaw the attainment of his Promised Land.
Bryce needed the incentive to make enough money for a
wife of expensive tastes before he hit his stride.

Requirements for success

Hard work

Study after study points to the need of *intelligent* hard
work to succeed in salesmanship. (What line of work doesn't
demand hard work to be preeminent in it?) Any man who
sells to make a "quick buck" isn't a professional salesman.
If there's a secret to success in selling then it's a simple and
obvious one: the deep desire, the strong will, the unfailing
interest to work hard to make a success.

This, of course, means more than mere busyness. Thousands of mediocre salesmen faithfully spend eight and more
hours every day calling on customers. (Unquestionably
they make more sales than if they made the same kind of
calls six hours a day.) Yet they don't succeed as they should
because of a grave lack. They lack the capacity (or don't
use it) to make each sales call a better one than the previous
call. Their great hindrance is complacency. They go

through the motions without profiting from their experience. They exercise their big muscles more than their brains.

It is the spark of the will to succeed that distinguishes the professional salesman. This spark, ignited in a thousand different ways—as exemplified by Eric Johnston, Sidney Moser, Rex Stout, Tom Bryce—makes the professional salesman.

For it sets him apart. It carries him over the rough spots. It helps him surmount all obstacles. It allows him to be himself (but, remember, himself at his best.) It compensates for many a personal shortcoming. It takes him to the top of the sales force—to promotion (if he wants it) to executive responsibility. It makes him willing to do well those details that hold little interest for him—such as writing reports. If he has it, all the other factors of success are ordinarily within his reach. Without it, he might just as well close up shop on a selling career. It was Edgar F. Roberts who said, "Every human mind is a great slumbering power until awakened by keen desire and by definite resolutions to do."

Common sense—intelligence—learning capacity

"Common sense," said William James, "is not sense common to everyone but sense in common things." In his contacts with customers, supervisors, and colleagues, the salesman has constant opportunity to apply common sense (C.S.)—through observation. How do the successful ones act, speak, think, influence others? The unsuccessful ones?

He thinks through his suggestions before he gives them. He weighs each of them by the questions: "Is it reasonable?" "Will it work?" "What makes it worthwhile?" And in the management of his sales territory he can also develop his C.S. Does he do first things first? Does he find ways to master details rather than let them swamp him? Does he constantly improve his work habits?

His intelligence is marked by adaptability. He likes new challenges. He profits from mistakes—doesn't repeat the same ones. He learns through trial and success, as well as trial and error. He enjoys solving problems—the practical ones that arise on the job. Ordinarily, he enjoys mental gymnastics, likes to do crossword puzzles or mental arithmetic.

Closely related is his learning capacity. Some sales positions demand a college degree, a kind of guarantee of learning capacity. Before joining a Johns Manville or IBM sales force, he may have to have an architect's or engineer's degree. Other companies demand a business or liberal arts degree—depending on the products or services sold. Many successful companies require no specialized academic training of the salesmen they hire. But all of them insist that their salesmen have learning capacity above the average. This is demonstrated by willingness to study and ability to profit from study. Beyond all else, the professional salesman should have—or should develop—a deep interest in reading, that gold mine of ideas.

Interest—self-confidence—enthusiasm

The professional salesman believes salesmanship offers more opportunity for him than other lines of work. He sees selling as a daily challenge. When asked why he's interested in selling, his typical replies are: "I like influencing others." "A customer is an opponent that I must vanquish." "I always think of a customer as a girl I want to persuade to marry me." "No two customers or sales interviews are alike." "The constant novelty of changing your strategy is what intrigues me."

William C. Dorr, well-known sales consultant, surveyed

a group of successful salesmen. He knew that the satisfactions a man finds in his career are seldom stated formally. He was particularly interested to get answers to the question: Why should I consider a career in sales?

Here's a sampling of the replies William Dorr recorded in man-to-man conversations. Notice the various causes of interest and enthusiasm for the profession in which the salesmen excel:

1. "I like to handle human chemicals."—E. J. McCORMACK, JR. (*United States Rubber Co.*)
2. "I gain a widening knowledge of industry."—GEORGE KRAKORA (*Wall St. Journal.*)
3. "Each day is a new ball game."—GEORGE V. DECKER (*The American Thread Co., Inc.*)
4. "I feel that I am building a business."—CLIFFORD J. KELLY (*C. H. Masland & Sons.*)
5. "I have learned the value of self-discipline."—FRANK E. HOLMES, JR. (*Encyclopaedia Britannica, Inc.*)
6. "A salesman becomes resourceful because he has to think on his feet, be ready with secondary moves.... There are objections and the prospect's status quo to be overcome. Is there any better way to develop a flexible mental capacity?"—J. M. VOLKHARDT (*Rit Division, The Best Foods Co., Inc.*)
7. "I believe a salesman's real asset is his roster of customers and prospects who like him, have profited from his ideas and thus become his friends. How can a man lose security like that?"—JACK FELDMAN (*Consolidated Lithographing Corp.*)

It is this deep-down interest that surmounts discouragement—gives him the basis of self-confidence and even enthusiasm.

Some successful salesmen report stage fright when they approach important customers, even after years of experi-

ence. But they don't show it. This very tension—as with
successful actors—holds them to high standards of performance. (At bottom both the accomplished salesman and
actor know they know their business.)

Studies show us that the surest way to build self-confidence is to increase and perfect techniques. The shy child
taught to dance well has more self-confidence at a party
than if he doesn't know how to dance. A salesman who
knows nine different ways to open a sales interview has
more self-confidence than one who has no planned opener.
And so the secret is to break down the job into its parts and
master each part. This done, self-confidence, interest, enthusiasm in the job grow. Easy? Not usually. But it's done
in salesmanship and other fields every day by the resolute
and mature.

The key to the kingdom

A.J. Cronin, author of *Keys of the Kingdom, The Cita-
del*—and many other works—had no idea of technique
when he started his first novel. He found it difficult to express himself. He struggled for hours over a single paragraph. "A sudden desolation struck me like an avalanche,"
he writes of this period. "I decided to abandon the whole
thing." Cronin threw away his manuscript. Shamed by a
Scottish crofter, he dug his papers out of an ash can, dried
them, and went doggedly to work. In three months of what
he calls "ferocious effort" he finished his novel *Hatter's
Castle,* and his publisher sold millions of copies.

H. W. Meyer, great salesman—obsessed that his early
salesmanship was marred by an inability to look big customers in the eye—spent a half-hour every night in a dark-
ened room seated before a large mirror. On each side of
the mirror was a lighted candle. Meyer looked steadily at
himself through the long half-hours. "Gradually," he says,

"I noticed I was looking at my customers as steadily as if they were the immobile image in the magic mirror."

Where there's a will, the professional salesman finds a way.

Communication skills

In the old days a salesman was supposed to have a gift of gab. Today mere word flow is under the gravest suspicion in the world of responsible buyers. Salesmen having it should learn to control it. For salesmanship is a give-and-take affair. We shall see in another chapter how intelligent listening is often more persuasive than a lot of chatter.

Of course, the salesman should learn—if he hasn't learned it already—a lively sense of participation. He should be comfortable to talk with. His speech should be free of "fawncy" sounds and distracting mannerisms—should not draw attention to itself but to the ideas and feeling it conveys. Ordinarily, it should conform to the standard of pronunciation used by the educated people of his territory. He should speak simple, lively words—the kind advertising copywriters use to attract readers. His words should always be easy for the customer to understand, should be stimulating. The gypsies have a word, *lavengro,* meaning "word master," that fits the professional salesman. For he too is devoted to the magic of words. The late great adman, Arthur Kudner, wrote to his son, "Never fear big long words. Big long words name little things. All big things have little names. Such as *life* and *death, peace* and *war.* Or *dawn, day, night, hope, love, home.* Learn to use little words in a big way. It is hard to do. But they say what you mean. When you don't know what you mean, use big words. That often fools little people."

H. Louis Thompson, president of Lehigh Coal and Navigation Company, emphasizes that sometimes the right word is worth more than a thousand pictures. And in selling and advertising, the difference between the right word and the almost-right word, according to Leo Burnett, can be the difference between *interest* and *disinterest, believing* and *disbelieving, sale* and *no sale!*

As for slang, when the salesman uses it, he should know that he's using it—and for a purpose. What's more, his voice should be flexible and resonant—to allow him to convey nuances of meaning. That's why most training programs for professional salesmen include voice recordings and speech training.

Throughout his career the professional salesman profits from training in formal public speaking. Often he's called upon to persuade groups of distributive salesmen to promote his products rather than his competitors'. Sometimes he participates in conferences and panel discussions. Increasingly, he makes joint calls to present ideas—with his executives—to buying committees. The more adept he is in participating in such situations, the better are the impressions he makes—the more selling does he do.

Added to all these speech techniques is the important one of writing simply—letters (both business and personal), reports, and memos. A book, such as Rudolph Flesch's *The Art of Readable Writing* (Harper & Brothers, New York) holds for the professional salesman many a practical hint to help him improve his letters and reports.

Persuasion—conviction

The professional salesman keeps in mind that persuasion is a fine and complicated art—a kaleidoscope of logic, emotional appeal, and personality impact. He therefore knows by rote all the benefits and advantages of the products or services he sells. He presents them from the customer's point of interest. He doesn't argue, for he knows the wisdom of the phrase: "A man convinced against his will/ Is of the same opinion still." Rather, he skillfully presents reasons for buying. What does this mean?

It means principally, attracting and holding the customer's attention, making knowledgeable use of one or more buyer motives, phrasing selling points in language of conviction and enthusiasm.

Try this in a lackluster monotone: "I *think* you'll like this item because it has merit."

Now try this with conviction and enthusiasm: "I *know* you'll want this wonderful product [name it], Mr. Jacob, because it has a 100 per cent markup and gives you a minimum of three turnovers a week in your streamlined stores!"

Which do you like better? Which will your customer prefer? Which is more likely to sell him?

Here is where conviction comes in: You must believe what you say. If the product is shoddy, don't sell it. Sell something else for a firm of quality products. Make sure of your facts about turnover, relate them to actual cases. Don't call his stores streamlined if they're not. Substitute another compliment based on fact. Finally, notice the fine but impressive differences such as between "think" and "know"; between using the customer's name and its omission, etc. This kind of analysis helps the salesman to keep his communication skills polished.

Sincere—sincerity

Some years ago a novel dealing with Madison Avenue made much use of "sincere" in a derisive sense. The leading character wore a "sincere tie," etc. Perhaps we should trace the word's pedigree to point up its noble qualities. For a professional salesman without sincerity is like a rope of sand.

More than 2,000 years ago Rome was an undistinguished-looking city whose buildings were mostly wood or brick. As she grew in power and wealth, her rulers wanted the public buildings to be grand. First the senators, then later the Caesars, rebuilt much of Rome. Instead of brick or wood, they chose stone or marble.

Some of those who sold marble to the Roman state weren't honest. They had their slaves rub wax into the cracks of marble slabs, blocks, and pillars. After they did this the marble seemed perfect. But when the weather beat upon the wax, it washed away, and the cracks reappeared.

And so the Senate passed a law: All marble sold for public buildings must be *sine cera*. That is, without wax. (As you may know, in Latin *sine* means "without"; *cera*, "wax.") In other words, the marble must be sound, whole; it must be what it appeared to be when bought. Anyone selling waxed marble after that was severely punished.

Sine cera many centuries later became "sincere" in our language to describe a person. Therefore, the salesman who is honest, frank, genuine—who is what he presents himself to be—is sincere. The professional salesman prides himself on his sincerity. It is the basis of his human relations and character. When real, it shines through.

Creativity

Standard Oil's Training Division has been doing research to identify the creative salesman (and other employees). Here are the main findings:

1. He's sensitive to problems and needs.
2. He looks for better ways of doing things.
3. He usually gets a wide variety of thoughts.
4. He can easily drop one line of thought and take up another.
5. He has breadth of vision.

6. He sees relationships between seemingly remote things and brings them together in meaningful ways.

Notice how the discoveries of Research Institute of America, Inc., as reported by Joseph D. Arleigh, confirm Standard Oil's findings:

1. He notices problems and situations that have previously escaped attention.
2. He tends to have many alternate thoughts on any given subject.
3. He relates to his work problem ideas that he has encountered elsewhere.

To those who may think they have little creative ability, Dr. Edwin R. Ghiselli, research psychologist at the University of Southern California at Berkeley, has some reassuring words. Dr. Ghiselli, in the study of creativity, concludes that creativity is more closely linked to initiative than intelligence.

The salesman who sets his mind to work along creative lines gets much fun from his work—and many rewards from doing so.

Assignment

Answer the following questions as objectively as you can:

1. Do you apply the elements of creative thinking to your work—as defined by the discoveries of Standard Oil and Research Institute of America?

2. Do you plan your own activities rather than wait to be told what to do?

3. Do you constantly seek better ways of handling all aspects of your responsibilities?

4. Do you adjust your working hours to meet the demands of your job without thinking of *overtime?*

5. Do you adjust grievances through proper channels, avoiding grumbling and complaining?

6. Do you hold inviolate the confidences placed in you by management, customers, and others?

7. Do you always reflect pride and satisfaction in your work?

8. Do you always consider the effect of your actions on the welfare of others?

9. Do you constantly seek to improve your skills, knowledge, and understanding?

10. Do you take full responsibility for the results of your own efforts and actions?

11. Do you fulfill all agreements entered into with others?

12. Are you loyal to your fellow salesmen, management, and company—never downgrading them by deed or word?

13. Is your chief work objective to render service?

14. Do you develop new ideas, plans, approaches, and share them with your fellow salesmen?

15. Do you strive for personal promotion only on the basis of superior performance?

"Red" Blaik's seven pillars of wisdom

West Point's famous football coach Col. "Red" Blaik gives a number of maxims to his winning team. The professional salesman finds them pertinent to his work:

1. A relaxed player performs best. A sense of humor and good fun keep one relaxed.
2. There never was a champion who to himself was a good loser. There's a difference between a good sport and a good loser.
3. Without ambition and enthusiasm for your work, the parade will pass you by.

4. Good fellows are a dime a dozen but an aggressive leader is priceless.
5. Games are not won on the rubbing table.
6. Inches make the champion, and the champion makes his own luck.
7. There is no substitute for work. It's the price of success.

3

How to Find Marketing-minded Companies to Work For

Mind the company you keep!

THEODORE H. SILBERT

Partners for the long pull

As you may know, salesmen traditionally have had a high divorce rate—higher than any other vocations or professions except actors, musicians, barkeepers, and firemen. Salesmen also have one of the highest rates of labor turnover. One cause of their high divorce rate and turnover is their tendency to whirlwind courtships. They don't take time enough to learn to know and cultivate the right partner.

The professional salesman, however, arranges things differently. He doesn't lose his head in the pursuit of a mate or position. He prides himself—and justly so—on his maturity. He takes the time to be certain he's making an excellent choice—one to endure and benefit all those involved. His concern is to find and work for a company that

30

cares about the climate it provides. For unless he works in an environment favorable to his ideals and capacities, he can't succeed as he should. He remembers that he'll spend more of his life working than in any other activity. Since he must look for a position, he seeks one with opportunity for growth. He avoids those where frustration and mediocrity prevail. He plans his approach intelligently. Among the bases he touches in winning the game are these— stated as directives:

Study the company's position in the economy and in its industry

One helpful way to do this is to measure the company by standards such as those provided by the American Institute of Management. As you may know, this nonprofit organization evaluates companies for investors and others. Here are its appraisal standards based on a point system:

1. Economic function: The part which the company plays in its industry and in the national economy. Excellent rating = 300 to 400 points.
2. Corporate structure: The orderly flow of authority and the effectiveness of executive communication. Excellent rating = 375 to 500 points.
3. Health of earnings: Growth in recent years and satisfactory experience through a full business cycle. Excellent rating = 460 to 600 points.
4. Service to stockholders: Stability of dividends at reasonable levels; regular growth in net worth; protection of invested capital from unnecessary risks. Excellent rating = 525 to 700 points.
5. Research and development: Actively engaged in a planned program of research for new ideas and products. Excellent rating = 525 to 700 points.
6. Directorate analysis: Degree to which the greater number

of directors are drawn from outside the company and are young and vigorous in their approach to business. Excellent rating = 675 to 900 points.

7. Fiscal policies: Sound financial management, pricing policies; preservation of working capital levels; avoidance of overly burdensome debt. Excellent rating = 825 to 1,100 points.

8. Production efficiency: Reducing operating and other costs and increasing the productivity of the labor force; maintenance of satisfactory labor relationships. Excellent rating = 975 to 1,300 points.

9. Sales vigor: The drive with which markets are exploited and the kind of sales techniques being used. Excellent rating = 1,050 to 1,400 points.

10. Executive evaluation: The team must work together in harmony; must be active in developing its successor management through training programs, not by hiring family relatives or by pirating outside executives. Excellent rating = 1,800 to 2,400 points.

To be rated an *excellent* company, the minimum number of points is 7,500; the maximum number possible is 10,000 points. Note well that *sales vigor* and *executive evaluation* receive the highest values.

Here are a few companies American Institute of Management assigns more than 9,000 points: CIT Financial, Du Pont, General Motors, Grand Union, IBM, Minnesota Mining and Manufacturing, National Cash Register, Procter & Gamble, Standard Oil of New Jersey. There are many others.

Look for a marketing-minded company

The marketing function is all encompassing. Its responsibility ranges from product (or service) conception, through development, testing, manufacturing to the customer, and beyond, even to teaching the customer how to consume.

The marketing-minded company

An example of foresight of a marketing-minded company is Westinghouse Electric Corporation. Here's a company looking twenty years ahead. Because its management discerned a declining rate of growth for its business, it called on its marketing people to start reversing the course of its future history. Result: The concept of the *total electric home* (T.E.H.)—the dream house just around the corner.

As you probably know, electric utility loads and capacity double every ten years. But two decades from now, it doesn't seem that they will. To make sure they do, Westinghouse is getting busy on a vigorous marketing program.

Westinghouse marketers foresee that the home is the most promising source of that new load—to keep the growth rate expanding. Westinghouse expects its T.E.H. concept to make two contributions to its corporate vigor: to expand sales of its consumer products division; to keep its shops busy manufacturing turbines, generators, and transformers.

Notice how a marketing concept, such as T. E. H., spreads benefits—to Westinghouse and its employees; to the whole electric and allied industries; to the economy of the countries where Westinghouse manufactures; to that part of the world devoted to free enterprise. And don't forget the home owners who will have the higher standard of living among the comforts of the T.E.H.

Another example of a marketing-minded company is General Electric. Over the last dozen years it has applied this policy: Build market or customer appeal into the product from its inception. GE thinks of a salesman's contact with his customer as the last step in the marketing

effort. The first step begins before the first engineer draws
the blueprint. This was described in a recent annual report:

> This introduces the marketing man at the beginning rather
> than the end of the production cycle and integrates market-
> ing into each phase of business. Thus marketing, through
> its studies and research, will establish for the engineer, the
> designer and the manufacturing man what the customer
> wants in a given product, what price he is willing to pay, and
> where and when it will be wanted. Marketing (has) authority
> in product planning, production scheduling and inventory
> control, as well as sales distribution and servicing of the
> product.

The goals of business

A business has only one valid goal. It's to create customers and sell at a profit. Someone recently said, "Markets
are not created by God, nature, or economic forces. They
are created by businessmen. It is business action—in every
single case—that creates the customer."

This means the customer's king. Like the professional
salesman, all other forward-looking businessmen bow to
the customer. Professor Peter Drucker of New York University puts the idea this way: "Because it is its purpose to
create a customer, any business enterprise has two—and
only these two—basic functions; marketing and innovation."

In his presidential address before American Paper & Pulp
Association, John R. Kimberly said: "Actually *Marketing*
is so basic that it isn't just enough to have a strong sales
department and entrust marketing to it. Marketing is not
only much broader than selling, it is not a specialized
activity at all. *It is the whole business seen from the point
of view of its final result,* that is, from the customer's
point of view." And Paul Mazur and Prof. Malcolm P. Mc-

Nair have defined marketing as "the creation and delivery of a standard of living."

To quote Professor Drucker again: "Innovation may take the form of lower price. But it may also be a new and better product (even at a higher price), a new convenience or the creation of a new want. It may be finding new uses for old products. It may be innovation in marketing techniques."

The marketing-minded company, therefore, believes the customer's king; knows that the customer keeps the business thriving—by paying its bills, employees' wages, and stockholders' dividends. The customer's wants and decisions to buy determine the company's business and direct its future.

Needed: marketing-minded employees

To satisfy the customer, the company needs marketing-minded employees all along the line—from machine tender to traffic man, to office clerk, to salesman, to executive. The marketing-minded company needs gifted, trained, well-motivated people—constantly interested in making innovations in their jobs to build customer good will. Only in this way can all departments contribute to a more successful, a more dynamic, a more profitable company.

Perhaps you've heard the story of the man who asked two workmen what they were doing. One said, "I'm laying stone." The other said, "I'm helping to build a cathedral for people to worship God." The second man had the marketing concept. Most employees have to be trained to see how their work—however modest their operation is—contributes to their company's basic purpose.

To accomplish its purpose, the marketing-minded company trains and develops its employees in attitudes, actions, accomplishments. In other words, the marketing-minded company is education-minded. An outstanding American enterprise, International Business Machines, is such a company. At a stockholders' meeting, President Thomas J. Watson, Jr. announced, "A great deal of our effort over the past few years has been centered on education not only of our own people but of our customers and prospects. . . . In fact, our ability to train our own people and our customers . . . is one of the major successes of the IBM company."

Many other American and Canadian companies are marketing minded. They create the kind of atmosphere in which professional salesmen flourish. For in these companies, all efforts of all departments are aimed at the customer and his wishes. This builds the salesman's prestige; it gives him the backing of all departments in the company —manufacturing, traffic, credit, advertising, merchandising, etc.—to help him do his work with distinction. It is such a climate that the professional salesman seeks and helps create.

Choose a company with a manpower development program

Such a company provides its employees with opportunities to grow. It promotes its own people to positions of increasing responsibility, rather than seeking them elsewhere. The development program provides employees with opportunities of learning—to prepare themselves for more responsible positions and rewards.

Among the activities of such programs are coaching, job rotation, in-company courses, out-of-company courses, discussion and "brainstorming" sessions, correspondence study, decision-making opportunities, personal analysis, appraisal programs, encouragement to participate in professional organizations.

Aggressive companies base their manpower development programs on this realization: Everyone has a vast untouched potential; in every sizable sales force—and other departments—there's a wealth of future executives. Further, they realize that when they promote from within the company, they give every ambitious employee added incentive to work hard; they build loyalty to company; they select those who know the company and its policies. Experience and study convince them that manpower development programs are a highly profitable investment.

How do you go about finding companies that meet the three prescriptions? Here are several hints:

How to find them

1. Get a list of the largest companies. (For example, once each year *Fortune* publishes a list of the 500 largest.)

2. Inquire about their policies. You can write them directly. Most of them have public relations departments; all of them have personnel divisions. You can address a letter of inquiry to either director of public relations or director of personnel.

You can also learn about company management and policies by making inquiries at a brokerage firm. Select a firm that is a member of the New York or Toronto Stock Exchange, if possible. It has—or will get for you—answers to most of your questions.

3. Talk with salesmen of these companies—or responsible businessmen who do business with them. They can tell you much of interest and value to you.

4. Be alert to the recruitment programs of marketing-minded companies. Most of them send recruiters to colleges and universities looking for candidates.

5. Make use of local career-building and placement

bureaus. C. W. Post College of Long Island University is one of many that conducts a career-building center. Here one may get vocational analysis and guidance.

6. Use the same procedures in evaluating smaller companies. Each big company was once small. It grew because its leaders based company success and growth on policies such as we've reviewed. Many a small company provides the same climate of excellence for the professional salesman as the best of the large ones.

7. Adapt the policies of successful companies if you work for yourself as a professional salesman, selling on your own. Seize every opportunity to conduct yourself and your business—and to develop yourself—as a responsible businessman. You'll then provide your own climate to succeed as a professional salesman. For professional salesmanship offers you a goal to strike at and a ladder to climb.

4

How to Impress Your Company Favorably

The professional salesman believes in the inevitability of his own success.

E. W. FAIRWEATHER

They compete for your services

General Electric—one of the most successful marketing organizations in the world—has 14,000 salesmen and other marketers, about 27 per cent of its salaried employees. GE is just one of many companies that sees a sharp rise in its need for the most important marketing resource: People. To keep pace with the explosive growth in business predicted for the next decade, GE—and other forward-looking companies—foresees an increasingly important role for marketing.

Charles Rieger, GE's manager of Marketing Personnel Development Service, recently reported an inventory of marketing personnel—says GE's marketing force could reach a total of 19,400 in the next four or five years. This is an increase of 4,400. Added to this, GE will probably hire 4,000 marketing people to replace retirements and separations—over the next five years. Total manpower needs, then, may be 8,400 new GE marketers. This represents 60 per cent of GE's present force.

Such estimates—added to those of other large and small companies—point to a bright future for professional salesmen and other marketers.

C. E. Souders, Karolton Paper Co.'s sales manager, says: "The high-level salesman today is—as always—in great demand. As American business continues to grow in marketing-mindedness, the professional salesman's services are in a buyer's market. That is, he can pretty much take his choice of companies to work for."

How then do companies recruit professional salesmen? What procedures do they follow? What impresses them in an applicant? Answers to these questions make helpful suggestions to two kinds of salesmen: the beginner and the salesman who wants to upgrade his present position.

Make friends of successful salesmen

W. J. French, Kimberly-Clark Vice President Consumer Sales, reports the readiest source of supply. He says, "If you ask your successful salesmen, they'll recommend excellent candidates to you." That's why many companies question their own salesmen periodically for recommendations. Since birds of a feather flock together, excellent salesmen are likely to have high-caliber friends interested in the same work. These men often want to join more dynamic companies. An obvious hint to the seeker, therefore, is: Make friends with successful salesmen. Ask them to recommend you to their management.

Prepare an excellent resumé

When you use a well-prepared resumé, you can go beyond the range of personal contacts. (The resumé serves you whether your initial contact is "cold" or by recommendation of a friend.) It helps you to cross over into a new industry or transfer to another part of the country.

What should your resumé include? What should its format be?

Length: Two pages are the limit; one and a half pages are better; one page—if possible—is best.

Format: Type individual resumés. Duplicated copies sometimes make a wrong impression. Be sure to write an excellent letter to accompany the resumé. Address it to the individual company—to the attention of the right person.

Contents: Include personal information: (1) outstanding and professional accomplishments; (2) family and community background; (3) summary of your education; (4) details of club membership, hobbies, etc.; (5) a frank statement of your career objectives; (6) your work experience chronologically listed—reversed in order; (7) references.

In a recent article in *Business Week* on the use of resumés in business, the editors made three suggestions—of interest to us here: Don't hide your age.—Don't bother with photographs. ("They mean little and may convey a negative impression.")—Don't hire a professional writer to compose your resumé. ("You're apt to wind up with a 'pat' job that will sound artificial.")

Make a good impression in the initial interview

The first interview—often held by recruiters at regional offices or at colleges and universities—lasts ordinarily from twenty to thirty minutes. Here the interviewer sizes you up. He's interested in weighing the impressions you make on him. Appearance, manners, speech are all tremendously important. He's impressed if you reveal some knowledge of his company, its products and policies. If you're looking for just a job, he may be interested—if he's manpower-short. But if you're looking for a position with *his* company—and give him specific reasons—you're more likely to clear this interview, the first hurdle.

And be sure to reveal yourself as a warm, interested person. NCR's Stephen Thrall exemplifies this point by telling about two applicants he interviewed. Both men had been stationed in Alaska in the Armed Forces.

Applicant A

Q: How did you like it up there?
A: I didn't.
Q: What did you do in your spare time?
A: Not much.

Applicant B

Q: How did you like it up there?
A: Oh! It was very interesting. Quite different from home. I learned to live with the cold, the snow, the ice—and liked it.
Q: What did you do in your spare time?
A: Why, we had a lot of fun for one thing. I remember one incident in the first week. We broke up a large wooden barrel. We used the staves as skis—until a shipment of real skis arrived. We worked off our boredom with snow-

ball fights, hunting and the like. And then there was
always plenty to read. Some of us organized *The Esqy
Thespies*. We had a grand time putting on skits, programs
for the holidays . . .

Applicant A never got beyond the first interview. Stephen
Thrall said it was hard to get more than a half-dozen words
out of the fellow. Moreover, his attitude was negative.
Applicant B went on to training school and became a great
producer of sales. He had (or developed) the conversational
sense of give and take, interests, enthusiasm, and a lot more
besides.

Take tests in your stride

Ordinarily, the next step is to take some psychological
tests. These usually include a test of general intelligence,
a measurement of your interests, various questionnaires.
If you've never taken such tests, you may want to get
some experience with them. Schools, colleges, universities,
guidance clinics all over the country extend testing services. When answering questions about yourself, be frank.
Otherwise you may be laying a trap for yourself.

Be prepared for the unexpected

Once you pass the initial interview and the tests, you'll
probably be given a series of interviews at the home office.
Anything can happen here. Some companies even adapt
the interview designed by Vice-admiral Hyman G. Rick-
over, the father of atomic submarines.

This can be as nerve-racking as the Chinese water tor-
ture. You're seated in a special chair—the front legs shorter
than the rear ones. Your eyes are blinded by the sun's rays
focused through Venetian blinds. Now comes the moment

of ordeal for a young Navy officer: the Admiral pulls the lanyard on a charge like this one: "Suppose you're on a sinking submarine with five other men. The conditions are that one, and only one, of you can be saved. Are you resourceful enough to talk the others into letting you be the man to survive?"

As soon as the candidate says, "Yes, sir," the Admiral brings five men into the room and says, "All right, son, start talking!"

In situations like this one, the candidate who keeps his sense of humor and does his best ordinarily makes a good impression.

Cooperate intelligently in the depth interview

Some companies have a carefully designed list of questions covered in a leisurely interview—or series of interviews. Three or more interviewers may divide these questions among them. Then each uses his questions when he interviews the candidate alone.

Less often, a committee interviews the candidate on the same questions. This is harder to take, say salesmen who have experienced both approaches.

In either event, the interviewers ask similar questions. The numbered items that follow are direct questions. Those in parentheses point to implications, and the interviewers don't ask them. But they indicate what the interviewers are really trying to explore. These are the ones that give the depth to the interview.

Introductory questions

    1. Is this address your home, Mr. _____?
       Where did you live before? How long?

(Lived at same place for reasonable period? If moves about unreasonably, is this a sign of instability?)

2. What kind of work are you looking for?

(Do we have that kind to offer him? If unemployed for some months—are his reasons favorable—such as looking for the right job? Or are they unfavorable—is he unrealistic in his demands? Has he had several jobs in the past two years? If so, may this not be a sign that he is unstable? Is his age favorable or unfavorable?)

Employment record

3. What experience have you had in the kind of work you want?

(Is this of value to us?)

4. What do (did) you do in a typical day in your present (latest) job?

(Of value to us?)

5. How did you get the job?

(Does his answer suggest resourcefulness, good planning? Or did someone get it for him?)

6. What did you do at first? Any promotions in rank or salary?

(Do his answers indicate good progress? Is he ambitious?)

7. What kind of outfit are they to work for?

(Does his reply reflect good attitude or griping? Is he realistic or emotional?)

8. What do (did) you like about the job? Dislike?

(How does his response reflect ability to get along with others? Fit into the organization? Would he fit into our organization? Does he show enthusiasm, drive? Are his dislikes justified? Is he mature in attitude?)

9. Why did you leave there?

(Lack of ability to do the job? Friction? Lack of reasonable opportunity? Work uncongenial *and* not suitable to his interests? Just restless and impatient?)

10. Where were you working before that?

(The interviewer asks questions similar to those above about each job. After considering all the applicant's jobs, he summarizes in his own mind by asking himself questions: Has he generally gotten along well with his supervisors and colleagues? Does he persist or give up easily if things are hard—as indicated by frequent job changes? Is he persevering or lazy? Reliable or unstable? In job changes, has he made his own decisions or depended too much on others?)

11. Which of your jobs did you like best? Why? The least? Why?
    (Do his reasons seem sound?)

12. What line of activity do you feel you have the most success in?
    (Related to selling?)

13. What kind of selling do you prefer?
    (Are his stated preferences well thought through?)

14. What would you like to be doing ten years from now?
    (Are his job interests favorable to our work? Does his experience show selling ability or probable aptitude? Does he have an understanding of customer problems? Does he have any skills we could use now?)

15. If you didn't have to work for a living, what would you like to do?
    (Mature attitude?)

16. Do you mind if we talk to your past supervisors about you?
    (Does he hedge?)

Military service

17. Would you like to tell me something about your service in the Armed Forces? What specifically did you do?
    (Did he show ambition to go up in the service? Military experience useful to our sales force? Evidence of getting along well with others? Did he show good self-improvement? Take responsibility?)

Education

18. What were you working toward in your schooling?
    (Did he have an occupational goal?)
19. What subjects did you like best? Least?
    (Interests significant to our kind of job?)
20. What were your grades like in your major subject?
    (Sufficient appropriate training? Evidence of ability to
    learn new work? Indications that he worked hard—
    saw things through—or quit in mid-term? Frank about
    failures?)
21. Did you have time for school activities?
    (Took vigorous interest? Tepid interest, though he had
    time available? Had to work instead?)
22. What extracurricular activities did you think were
    worthwhile?
    (Mature attitude? Experience of possible value to us?)
23. What offices, if any, did you hold?
    (Liked by others? A leader?)
24. How did you spend your summer vacations?
    (Profitable? Experience useful to us?)
25. Are you taking any courses now?
    (Ambitious? Course or courses of value to us?)

Outside activities since leaving school: Exclude Racial, Religious Groups

26. What do you do in your leisure time?
    (Prefer group activities? A lonely fellow?)
27. What business or professional clubs interest you?
    (Is he a mixer? Will he further our public relations pro-
    gram?)
28. Are you holding any offices now?
    (Does he take responsibility? Do others elect him to lead
    them?)
29. How often do these groups meet?
    (Good balance? Enough social life, but not excessive?)

30. What do you do in community affairs?
    (Good citizen? Social standing as indicated by activities too high or too low for job?)
31. How do you feel about taking a drink?
    (Sensible or poor judgment?)

General information

32. How many in family? Mother work?
    (Childhood normal or unhappy? Family background favorable or unfavorable?)
33. Plans for marriage? You have your own household? Any youngsters? How old?
    (Harmonious personal life or evidence of unstable emotional life at home? Does his family provide him with a powerful work incentive? Are his burdens overwhelming?)
34. What illnesses have you had?
    (Health a hazard?)
35. How is the family's health?
    (Source of worry?)
36. During the starting period, a salesman's income is rather limited. Are your finances in such shape that you could afford to begin working for us at $_____ a month?
    (In good financial condition? Or too heavily in debt? Insurance adequate, indicating sense of financial responsibility? Considering his financial status, will his earnings with us be attractive?)
37. What do you know about our company?
    (Evidence of real interest? Has he been intelligent about finding out about our business?)
38. What is there about this job with us that appeals to you?
    (Wants *a* job or *this* job?)
39. What does your wife (family) think about your working here?
    (A help or a hindrance? Indication of harmony or trouble at home?)

40. Would your wife be willing to move to a different part of the country? Would you?
    (Any hedging? Any geographical limitations? If so, are the reasons such that we would be willing to abide by them?)
41. Would your wife (family) object to your being away from home nights during the week?
    (How many?)
42. How are you about getting up in the morning?
    (A sleepy head?)
43. Can you stick to the job when you are on your own?
    (Do his reasons sound plausible?)
44. Would you and your family be willing to transfer?
    (House ownership or other complications?)

Character references

45. Who are your character references?
    (What kind of people vouch for him? Would he be congenial with our salesmen and customers?)

You find most interviewers of companies that hire professional salesmen personable. They treat you courteously. In return, they expect good manners, frank, intelligent responses to their queries. By reviewing such questions—and your answers to them—before you make your appearance, you can acquit yourself successfully.

Rate yourself on the interviewers' questionnaire

After they have interviewed you in depth, the interviewers ordinarily fill out a questionnaire about the impressions you made on them. If they concur, you're offered a position.

Such questions provide the applicant with an opportunity for self-appraisal. Several large companies—hiring professional salesmen—ask their interviewers to appraise the applicant's performance in the depth interview with these questions:

1. Was his conduct pleasant?
2. Did he show good judgment?
3. Did he ask intelligent questions?
4. Did he make a good appearance?
5. Does he have good voice and diction?
6. Is his cultural level suitable for us?
7. Did he have sufficient poise?
8. Did he have self-control?
9. Did he appear to be nervous, high-strung, cocky, bored, or condescending?
10. Did he give the impression of being fair-minded, honest with customers?
11. Did he leave the impression of being a man to keep his promises?
12. From the way he conducted himself, would you expect him to make a good sales presentation?

The company takes a wife

Alert companies discover that when they hire a salesman they also hire his wife; that unless she's in favor of her husband's work he can't succeed as he should. Increasingly, therefore, after the salesman surmounts the challenges of the initial interview, the tests, the depth interviews, a company representative interviews the salesman and his wife —usually in their home.

The company wants to make sure that:

1. The salesman's wife and his home will represent him as a professional man.
2. The wife gets a description of her husband's responsibilities.
3. She understands her husband's career with the company

    may require him and his family to move from one part of the country to another—sometimes frequently.

4. She may have to be alone some of the time, especially while her husband travels or attends meetings.
5. She's expected to encourage him to spend time at home on study and self-improvement.
6. Any questions she may have about the company and its policies are answered.

Experience proves that—even though the salesman is persuasive with his customers—he often fails to "sell" his wife about his work and company. It's a case of the shoemaker's children going barefoot. The company therefore makes sure that the wife knows about her husband's work plans before it hires him.

Some companies—once they establish the policy of interviewing applicants' wives—also send a representative to call on the wives of their salesmen. "If I had known," said the wife of a veteran salesman, "when Joe first started with the company the things I've learned in our chat tonight, I'm sure we could have avoided many tensions and misunderstandings."

This procedure reduces turnover, makes the salesman more productive, increases family understanding. Moreover, it makes the wife feel she's part of the team. It's a truism among sales managers that "When you hire a salesman you hire his whole family."

Sometimes during these at-home discussions, problems arise that the interviewer can help resolve. Examples are how to get a family budget started; how a wife can spend her time constructively—for instance, helping her husband with his paper work; how to overcome loneliness. Although companies can't afford to maintain a marital relations clinic, they're eager to extend what services they can in the promotion of worthy family life for their salesmen.

The interviewer reports his recommendation to the company. If the wife makes a good impression and she's in favor of her husband's application, the candidate is hired —after passing a physical examination, filling out records, and completing other details.

The training program

The days when the "new hire" was given a price list and a territory and told to "sink or swim" are as outmoded as a 1921 Model T. Competition won't permit it. Successful companies invest a lot of money to train their salesmen. Did you know that recent estimates indicate $12,000 as the average cost to recruit, select, train a salesman—before he begins to return the investment through sales? That's why turnover and careful training of salesmen cost so much.

Each company has its own distinctive program of training. Take Dick Wilson, a representative of Alcoa's sales force, as an example. He was carefully screened for his work —only 1 out of 66 candidates makes the grade at Alcoa. He's a graduate engineer. Before his first call he spent time in nine principal Alcoa plants to learn how aluminum is made and fabricated. Then the company gave him an intensive course in sales training and customer service.

Some companies assign a new salesman to accompany seasoned salesmen on their calls—for two or more weeks before he's given formal sales training in the company's classes. Other companies take their new salesmen through formal indoctrination and training programs before sending them with experienced salesmen.

Then there are the review courses and the periodic sales meetings. Like every other professional man, the salesman needs occasional refresher stints. Only in that way can he keep abreast of progress.

When he participates in company training programs he is open-minded and cooperative. For that way he learns best and profits most. He's wise enough to realize that management constantly evaluates his participation in the programs.

If he wants to prepare himself well for getting the most from the company programs he can profit from the results of a recent survey. Members of the Sales-marketing Executives of Chicago, Inc., say they would put emphasis on the following five courses if they were preparing for professional salesmanship now. The five are (1) public speaking, (2) psychology, (3) sales management, (4) English, (5) salesmanship. Interestingly, 88 per cent of the members of this club have some college training.

All training, of course, involves communication. That's why the salesman should excel in speech and writing before entering his training program.

The appraisal program

Perhaps the commonest question in the minds of all of us—pertaining to our work—is: How am I doing? It usually has a corollary: I wonder how the boss thinks I'm doing? To satisfy this just curiosity, intelligent sales management today has an appraisal program.

Twice a year or oftener the sales supervisor or manager sits down with his salesmen individually—to review the job that *both* of them are doing together. This provides an opportunity for a meeting of the minds. It also lets the salesman know his strength; his areas of indicated growth and improvement. It gives the salesman an opportunity to express his hopes and ambitions. It permits the supervisor to point out what the salesman must do to realize his ambitions. It allows the supervisor an opportunity to map out a program of self-improvement for the salesman to follow until the next appraisal interview. Finally, it reveals to the supervisor how he can be more helpful to the salesman.

Sometimes the sales supervisor records the appraisal on note paper; sometimes he fills out a formal outline; and sometimes he answers a printed questionnaire—whichever company policy sets. In any of the alternatives he covers the same ground. When he does the job well, he lets the salesman see what he writes about him—after they together decide what's to be written.

Here is a sample appraisal questionnaire which you may want to use in self-appraisal of the job you're doing.

Salesman's appraisal questionnaire

Personal characteristics

1. Do I rely on my efforts to get the job done, or do I lean on others for help?
2. Do I stick to a job until I accomplish my objectives, or do I give up easily?
3. To what extent can I be depended upon to give my total efforts to meet my responsibilities?
4. Am I cooperative in my attitude and actions toward company policy and management decisions or do I complain and seek special consideration?

Customer relations

5. Do most of my customers accept me as the personification of my company or as just another salesman?
6. To what extent does my manner with my customers create a desire on their part to hear and accept my suggestions enthusiastically?
7. How well do my customers cooperate in following my suggestions for improving their sale of our products?

8. Do I adapt myself to dealing with all types of customers or do I have difficulty adapting to certain types?

Leadership qualities

9. Am I a "self-starter" or do I need constant prodding to get things done?
10. In a crisis, to what extent do I remain calm and move against it, rather than become discouraged, rattled, or incapable of action?
11. Do I consistently create new and unique ways to handle my job or handle it by conventional methods without originality?
12. Do I make my own decisions—within the limits of company policy—for handling the problems of my territory or do I constantly ask, "What do I do next?"
13. How capable am I in getting work accomplished through others?
14. Do I intelligently direct the efforts of salesmen when they work under my guidance?
15. What is my evaluation of the attitude and morale of my customers?
16. Do my habits and actions reflect a desirable degree of self-control, or lack of restraint?
17. Do I plan my work in advance and then work my plan —using company forms, sales promotion plans, etc., as provided?

Sales ability

18. How well do I organize my sales presentation and aim it at the specific needs and interests of each customer?
19. Are my sales presentations effective? Do they get results?
20. Am I convincing and enthusiastic when giving my sales presentations?
21. How successful am I in getting the order or selling the idea?

22. Am I completely familiar with all conditions in my market or territory?
23. Do I keep myself and my customers abreast of conditions in the market?
24. Do I follow through on centrally planned programs, making use of all sales tools provided me? Or do I discard them, or just use certain ones?
25. Do I consistently handle my work in an organized way?
26. In what specific ways do I need to improve my speaking ability?
27. How can I improve my writing ability?

Summary

28. Considering all aspects of the job I am doing—what at this time are my outstanding abilities and qualifications?
29. What areas require improvement or at present are hindering my performance?
30. What plans have my supervisor and I made for supplying my present deficiencies?
31. What progress has my supervisor noted since the last appraisal?

If your sales supervisor doesn't give you an occasional appraisal, why not ask for one? This does a number of constructive things. It lets him know you are interested in doing better; it's a compliment to his leadership; it lets you know where you stand with him; it graciously forces him to do his job.

Humility is the noblest of them all

In all experiences the salesman has in getting started and working well with his company, nothing serves him quite so well as humility. If he's receptive and eager to learn; if he accepts procedures in good faith; if he cooperates in good heart—he'll make an excellent impression, do well, and have within him what Herbert Hoover calls "peace at the center."

W. Harold Rea, former salesman, had an interesting experience. Rea is president of Canadian Oil Companies, Ltd. He recently spoke before Toronto's National Sales Executives Club. He told how a company president hired a psychologist to examine the executives of his organization— including himself. The psychologist administered a battery of aptitude and personality tests and interviewed all the executives in depth. Then he wrote a report in which he stated bluntly the president was the main cause of the company's difficulties. He worried a lot about details, was stingy, unwilling to delegate authority, and too indecisive. Deeply distressed at the outcome, the president decided to retire. But his board of directors persuaded him to stay on and redefine the jobs of the other executives. When he did this, the other executives carried their responsibilities well. The president avoided day-to-day details. And of course company sales and profits climbed.

Harold Rea ended his speech by saying, "The company I have been talking about is my own. The chief executive I have been talking about was your speaker!"

PART 2

How Salesmen Can Sell More

5

Develop Right Habits
to Up Your Efficiency

> The less you know how to do your work,
> the harder it is to do.
>
> R. B. CASSINGHAM

A large part of a salesman's professional integrity consists in right work habits. Perhaps it was George Eliot who called a good habit "that beneficent harness of routine which enables successful men to live calmly yet accomplish much." The professional salesman establishes excellent work habits to get rid of aimless effort, to make his minutes and hours productive. They thus add much to his sense of personal achievement.

Some years ago Ralph Whitehead, office manager of International Cellucotton Products Company, did a study of work habits of salesmen—especially those dealing with paper work. In his recommendations to the salesmen, Ralph Whitehead wrote, "Efficient work habits increase your self-confidence. They enable you to approach your accounts secure in the knowledge that you have all the tools and information necessary to give them the best possible service."

Here are some suggestions that successful salesmen recommend. They are worth developing as habits.

Hints to help make your paper work easy

As a professional salesman you have to spend many hours preparing your sales presentations. You also have to invest a lot of time reporting your results. You have to keep records, constantly analyze your territory and accounts, write letters and memos, check data, file, submit expense reports, fill in data sheets and order forms, write daily and special reports, plan creative presentations, etc. Actually, you devote more time to paper work than you spend in the presence of the buyer. Results of surveys indicate that this is the experience of most salesmen who call on buyers.

Each company has its own demands regarding the kinds and amount of paper work its salesmen must do. You'll need to adapt the suggestions in this chapter to your company's policies. However, these suggestions are so essential that you'll find them applicable.

1. Do your paper work faithfully. As you know, most salesmen dislike clerical work. But it must be done. As a professional salesman, you'll see the necessity—the reason —for all the paper work you're asked to do. So you'll do it well and promptly. Don't look for excuses to avoid it or put it off. They're too easy to find.

A sales manager offered a prize to the salesman who turned in the best daily reports for six months. Twenty-two salesmen competed. The salesman who won the prize was a young father living in an apartment in Brooklyn. What with two babies, the four-room apartment was crowded. Every night after supper—when the dishes were done and the babies put to bed—the salesman brought in two orange crates from the fire escape. They were covered with oilcloth. He'd unwrap them and take out his files and records. Then he and his wife would work on them at the kitchen table. They averaged an hour of work together every night. Once finished, he'd wrap his materials in the orange crates and put them back on the fire escape. Just before going to bed he'd take the dog for a walk and drop the report in the mailbox.

The instance is an excellent foil for the excuse so often heard, "If I'd only have a den or an office, I'd be able to do my paper work on time!"

2. Don't let your paper work pile up for the week end. Keep on top of it daily. Working efficiently—away from the TV or radio, for instance—you should be able to maintain your paper work on one hour a day. If possible, set the same hour every day, for example, right after dinner. This gives you the evening for other things. Some salesmen who like to get up early do their paper work before breakfast.

3. Spend a few minutes before (and after) each sales call on the paper work involved. Often you'll find you can fill out order blanks, check route lists, keep accounts of inventory, note expense items, etc., in these short periods. This procedure helps you to make a better sales call. It also keeps much of your paper work current.

4. Make good use of the trunk of your car. A successful salesman who travels the state of Maine has his files and data neatly arranged in the back of his car. Here it's available while he's on the road. He uses his "office on wheels" throughout the day. At night, he does the final stint at his motel. Result is that on Saturdays he has to spend one hour only—on the average—to complete his weekly reports, filing, etc.

5. Keep excellent files. Your filing affects all your operations. You can buy inexpensive cardboard files or the more permanent steel cabinets preferably to accommodate 8½- by 11-inch sheets. The idea is to have a permanent place to keep correspondence, invoices, advertising mats and tear sheets, correspondence supplies, etc. Use an alphabetical index for ready reference.

6. Keep your filing system simple and logical. File by subject matter; avoid cross references. In your file cabinet you'll place some Manila folders. Don't keep too many of them. Relatively few will be more efficient. If the material in a folder becomes too bulky for quick reference, sort it. Put it into subheading folders. Put them behind the major subject index.

7. Sort out and throw away unneeded material once a week. Too often files become choked with useless matter. It slows you down. Make a good friend of your wastepaper basket.

8. Keep your files up to date. File and sort your material every day. This is the time to get rid of papers you no longer need.

9. Keep two main categories of material: the matter you need to take with you every day and the materials you keep at home for record or storage purposes. Even if you carry all your files in the trunk of your car, the two suggested categories will boost your efficiency.

10. Try to keep your subject headings few as possible. These headings are recommended for a salesman's filing system. You may wish to adapt them to your needs. Following are twenty sample file headings:

a. *Account Records:* These include invoices, sales reports, routine correspondence.

In metropolitan territories you may want to keep an

individual file folder for each of your accounts. Group
the folders by class of accounts: dealers, jobbers, industrial accounts, etc. Alphabetize each class of accounts and
file in individual account folders.

If you have a traveling territory, keep a folder for each
town. Separate them by your routes. Arrange your accounts alphabetically—by class of accounts—and put
them in a town folder. Treat larger towns like a metropolitan territory.

b. *Advertising:* File your current advertising matter that you
can't file under the other headings here, for example,
newspaper and magazine schedules, mailings, TV and
radio scripts.

c. *Appointments:* These you can ordinarily file under
"Follow-up."

d. *Competitive Activity:* Here you file your carbons of reports on the activity of your competition.

e. *Customer Data Sheets:* Keep whatever forms you may
have on your customers' orders with your "Account
Records."

f. *Daily Reports:* Ask your sales manager how long you
must keep copies of your daily reports. Throw them away
as soon as they've served their purpose.

g. *District Manager:* Keep in this folder those matters you
need to take up with your district manager the next time
you see him.

h. *Expenses:* File copies of your daily or weekly expense reports, also correspondence relating to them. Throw them
away as soon as they've been approved.

i. *Fleet Car:* If your company provides you with a car,
keep here all matters referring to it. If you provide your
own car, keep the information under "Car."

j. *Follow-up:* Carry this folder with you at all times. (Some
salesmen prefer to call it "Do It Today," "Current,"
"Pending," or "Follow Through.") It's a constant re-
minder of urgent business. Include in it commitments,

promotional materials, promised orders, adjustments to
be made, etc. After you handle each item, discard it or
file it under its usual subject heading.

As part of your "Follow-up," keep a daily diary. This
you ordinarily carry in your pocket. "Do It Today" or
"Week at a Glance Jr." are well-known brand-name
diaries you can buy at a stationery store. Use your diary
to record appointments, telephone numbers, addresses,
and like information.

  k. *Forms:* Most companies supply their salesmen with forms
     —order blanks, expense reports, inventory control, sales
     reports, etc. Take some with you; keep a supply at home.
     Order supplies before you run out of them.

  l. *Personal:* This folder is your own. Put into it your income
     tax returns, check stubs, hospitalization records, mort-
     gage payment and insurance receipts, etc.

 m. *Price Lists:* Keep a good supply of these. Discard out-
     moded lists when new ones are issued.

  n. *Quotas:* Here you include your sales performance versus
     quotas and related information.

  o. *Route Lists:* Keep them up to date, either in a folder or
     on 3- by 5-inch cards. See Chapter 7.

  p. *Sales Bulletins:* Your sales bulletins are likely to multiply
     throughout the year. When one deals with a particular
     subject, index it under its subject heading. Keep those of
     general, nonspecialized subject matter all alphabetized
     under "Sales Bulletins."

  q. *Sales Reports:* Use this folder to keep your reports that
     cover your territory as a whole. Your reports on your in-
     dividual accounts you keep in your "Account Records."

  r. *Sales Training:* If your company has an elaborate sales
     training program—or if you're engaged in one on your
     own—you may need subfolders on product information,
     public speaking, creative selling, sales analysis, etc. Other-
     wise one folder on this subject will be enough.

  s. *Statistics:* In this folder you keep pertinent data about
     the progress of your industry, company, etc. A steel or

coal salesman, for example, would keep his tonnage reports in this folder.

t. Trade Papers: Important articles, advertisements, news items from the trade papers you read—go into this folder.

These 20 items should give you a simple system for filing. You may want to add—or drop—a few items. Stay away from general captions, such as "Correspondence" and "Miscellaneous." They become catchalls and defeat the purpose of a ready-reference file. You may want to make one other addition: include a folder for "Ideas" or "Sales Ideas." Here would go any tidbit that you collect from reading, conversation, contemplation. You'll find it valuable for presentations, promotions, or visual aids.

Handle correspondence promptly

Answer your correspondence daily. Then the matters are fresh in your mind. Don't let it pile up. Type it. Many companies supply their salesmen with portable typewriters. If your company doesn't, you'll probably want to invest in one of your own. And if you don't know how to type, you'll be amazed how fast you can learn—even when you use the hunt-and-peck method. In the business world, typing is always preferable to scribbling—to avoid misunderstanding and speed up reading—especially in these times when handwriting has fallen on evil days.

To help the salesman save time and sighs, some companies provide him with a dictating machine. At the end of the workday the salesman mails the tape or platter to the office. Here the typist puts it into final form. Other companies encourage their salesmen to telephone their dictation of reports and correspondence to a regional office. You see, time is of the essence. The professional salesman uses it with care.

If your territory demands a lot of travel, request your company mail clerk to allow one day's delay in posting your material while you're on the road. This helps to prevent missed mailings. They sometimes take weeks to catch up with you. Promptness is the habit for correspondence!

Take excellent care of company property

Modern psychology teaches us that we are constantly *projecting* the personality. The clothes we wear, how we decorate our homes, our choice of mates—all are examples of personality projection. That's why the appearance of the salesman's car, his sales kit, his advertising mats, etc., bespeak his personality. To reflect himself favorably, he therefore keeps his car washed and in good repair. If he carries advertising mats, he doesn't keep too many of them in the trunk of his car. He doesn't want them soiled or damaged. He may put them into a corrugated carton, protected and neatly arranged. Likewise his sales kit is spick and span— its contents in apple-pie order. This helps him carry on a deft presentation, simply because he doesn't have to root for an item while he's talking. His fingers find it without breaking his customer's attention. And if he uses merchandise in the sales presentation, he makes sure it's fresh and attractive.

Why not take inventory of company property in your care? Put it into first-rate condition and keep it that way. It helps you to make the right impression on customers, ups your efficiency, contributes to your euphoria, the psychologist's tall term for sense of well-being!

Get help to break annoying little habits

Many of us develop irritating habits unknowingly— habits that detract from professional deportment. They may range from dirty fingernails to chewing gum while talking, from head scratching to slovenly diction. A basic reason we don't get rid of them is that we can't see or hear ourselves as others see or hear us.

One way to break a demon of this sort is to enlist the help of a friend. A Chicago salesman recently reported the following experience of two friends:

JOE: Jack, I've got a proposition for you. The boss said I drop some of my word endings. He says I say *goin'*, *runnin'*, *talkin'* for *going, running, talking,* etc. I guess I've always talked like that. How's for helping me break the habit? Call it to my attention every time you hear me say it— when we're alone.

JACK: Okay. But only if you'll do something for me. Tell me, do I have a similar habit?

JOE: No, but since you've asked for it, I notice you flick your cigarette ashes on the floor—even when a tray's handy.

JACK: Never thought about it. I don't have a wife to nag me like you married fellows. Okay, it's a deal. Let's remind each other.

JOE: Well now, let's make it interesting. Every time I catch you, you pay me a dime. Every time you catch me, I'll fork up.

Within two weeks Joe and Jack helped each other to break two distracting habits at a cost of $2.10 and $1.50, respectively.

Of course, you can also ask your supervisor to check up on your habits (if he doesn't already do so) or a member of the family. In this way you ensure yourself against the stealthy encroachments of annoying little habits all of us may contract.

Keep healthy

As the result of periodic health examinations—now given by many companies—we've learned a good deal

about salesmen's health. Here are some conclusions made
by company physicians:

1. Salesmen (and executives) ordinarily begin their careers
   with abundant health—far above the national average.
   Because of travel; irregular hours of sleep; unwise eating,
   smoking, and drinking habits; working under tension—
   they develop more health problems than people in many
   other vocations and professions.

2. There's a vast and vital difference between excellent,
   buoyant health and the health of the average person or
   one who is only well enough to be out of bed. And a definite relationship exists between high health and excellent
   sales records on the one hand; between lowered health
   and sales slumps on the other. (This finding leads companies to invest a lot of money in preventive medicine
   and health education among their salesmen.)

3. Their point of view is psychosomatic. That is, an emotionally distressed salesman is bound to have physical up-
   sets and, vice versa, body discomforts and diseases affect
   the attitudes and emotions of those afflicted. "A sound
   mind in a sound body" is as honored a motto today as it
   was 2,000 years ago.

4. If the salesman sets six basic health habits early in his
   career—and adheres to them faithfully—he need not
   fear becoming incapacitated soon after middle life or
   dying between fifty and sixty years of age—the decade of
   most frequent deaths for salesmen and executives.

5. The six basic health habits are:
   a. A lot of fresh air every day, preferably in the sunlight.
   b. Regular but not strenuous exercise—especially for
   salesmen who drive cars or ride planes, buses, or trains
   in their daily work.
   c. Good food and wise eating habits. (Keep your weight
   down.)
   d. Enough rest and regular hours of sleep. (As much as
   you need.)

e. Wholesome attitudes toward self and others. (Rout fear, worry, and hatred out of your life.)

f. A thorough physical check-up at least once a year.

The healthy mind

Dr. Karl A. Menninger of the famed Menninger Clinic writes, "Let us define mental health as the adjustment of human beings to the world and to each other with a maximum of effectiveness and happiness. Not just efficiency or just contentment—or the grace of obeying the rules of the game cheerfully. It is all these together. It is the ability to maintain an even temper, an alert intelligence, socially considerate behavior, and a happy disposition. This, I think, is a healthy mind."

The mature mind

In his great book *The Mature Mind*—well worth every professional salesman's careful reading—Prof. Harry A. Overstreet says, "Our first need is to realize that every situation in life offers its opportunity for mature or immature responses. We do not have to wait for special occasions." How true this is of the professional salesman's daily challenges! Perhaps the basic test of his maturity is to seek expert help when and if he becomes emotionally distressed. For an upset solar plexus is as amenable to correction as is the flu or malfocused eyes. Habits that lead to "the peace that passeth understanding" are the kind the professional salesman develops.

6

How to Get the Most Out of 24 Hours a Day

> Hold fast to the present hour. Every state of duration, every second, is of infinite value.
>
> GOETHE

In the world of work and personal advancement, time is a professional salesman's best friend. How he values it and how he uses it determine his success and happiness. Along with the power of speech, the time sense is the most distinctive mark of human intelligence. But it must—like speech—be learned and used.

"Mañana"

On the island of Borneo—in the Kingdom of Sarawak—the missionaries were puzzled. They would ring the bells of their churches to notify the gentle natives of services. Sometimes the natives would come long after the signal. Sometimes they would arrive a day or two early—would sleep in the churches—awaiting the services. They were always interested. The missionaries discovered that the natives ate, slept, worked as they individually pleased. Time, as we know it, was foreign to them. Only after patient teaching did the natives learn the meaning of a set time.

As you know, animals respond in a reflexive sort of way —to the seasons, the sunrise, the sunset, moonlight, and darkness. They set up a rhythm of life that marks off periods —time.

Sharpen your time sense

The more complex your civilization, the more dependent you are on time. You have to develop an acute appreciation of cycles—years, months, weeks, hours, minutes, seconds and—in scientific undertakings and sports events—microseconds. Otherwise, you can't compete with those who do have it.

On the basis of the time sense, a salesman can build a fascinating life and career—full of worldly success as well as inner peace and outward calm. His first challenge is to develop a sense of the *value* of time and the realization that it's basic to efficient work and health. T. S. Eliot, in his great poem "The Wasteland," has a haunting refrain:

Hurry up! Hurry up!
There is time.
There is time.

What does it mean to you? John Wesley said, "I always make haste, but am never in a hurry."

Sales managers constantly urge their salesmen to make wiser use of their time. Some salesmen take the advice. Others continue to dawdle in mediocrity. Psychologists tell us that this latter group doesn't really understand the anatomy of time, has an underdeveloped time sense. And therefore they don't respond to the advice.

Valuable time concepts

One way for all of us to develop a deeper reverence for time is to review some concepts. That way we can get more good out of the rules—can make the most of advice on how to use time wisely.

Most of us understand that time is relative. A second spent on a red-hot stove seems vastly longer than the same time spent on a comfortable sofa. Yet, according to the stop watch, the actual time spent on each is exactly the same.

Rub a nose on a diamond mountain

Let's also agree that time may become so extensive that we can't comprehend it. Take eternity, for instance. It begins and ends at the same place—nowhere. To try to understand it, we have to turn to an analogy. Suppose that a salesman—just once in his lifetime—rubs his nose against a Pikes Peak of pure diamond (one of the hardest substances). And then suppose his son once in *his* life does the same thing—rubs his nose once against a diamond Pikes Peak. Finally, suppose the salesman's grandson does likewise, and so on down the corridors of time—each generation sending an SOS (son of a salesman) to rub his nose once against the diamond mountain. When Pikes Peak is worn away by only nose rubbings, then we might say one second of eternity is gone.

But enough of this philosophical speculation! Let's turn to more reasonable concepts. How about the stars? As you know, they're so far away we refer to their distances by light-years. Now light, you'll recall, travels at about 186,000 miles a second. A light-year, therefore, is about 6 trillion miles. For example, the time light takes to travel from here (the earth) to Alpha Centauri—the star nearest us—is 4.3 light-years, or 25 million, million miles. Breathtaking, isn't it?

Time, as geologists see it, is old too, but just a grain of sand in the hourglass compared with star time. They estimate our oldest rocks are less than 2 billion years—just plain, everyday years, not light-years.

But hold on, the history of man is not much more than 7,500 years. Among man's oldest monuments are the Sphinx and Pyramids of Cheops—built about 5,000 B.C. Why, we're just in our swaddling clothes!

Life on earth has a rather narrow time band. Perhaps the oldest living animals are deep-sea turtles. Some of them now living were born in Shakespeare's day. The oldest members of the plant kingdom—some bristlecones in California's White Mountains—have been growing for more than 4,600 years.

At the other end of the scale, we have amoebae and paramecia—one-celled animals that live their cycle in seconds. Sales executive John M. Besser—in stressing to his salesmen the importance of time—tells them about an experience he had in a biology class.

Jack Besser took a drop of water from a stagnant tank, put the drop on a slide, put the slide under the lens and saw countless little creatures. Then he left the lab for a quick cigarette. When he returned, he looked again. They had died.

In comparison with light-years our own life span is just as fleeting as the amoeba's. It's this thought that turns all serious, high-minded salesmen to make the most of each day. It is the same thought that the sages of many civilizations accent so often. In the days when Hindu civilization was very young, an unknown wise man composed a lesson on this theme:

Listen to the exhortation of the Dawn.
Look to this day.
For it is life, the very life of life,
In its brief course lie all the verities
And realities of your existence.
The bliss of truth, the glory of Action.
The splendor of Beauty.
For yesterday is but a dream
And tomorrow is only a vision.
But today,
Well-lived, makes yesterday
A dream of happiness
And every tomorrow a vision of hope.
Look well, therefore, to this day.
Such is the Salutation to the Dawn!

Let's return to the time sense. In sleep it's quite different
from when we awake. You may have had the dream of
falling. You seemed to fall forever—until the floor came
up to meet you halfway as you fell out of bed. Psychologists
say you begin to dream of falling as you start to fall. In
your dream, the fall seems interminable because your sense
of time is different when you sleep from when you are
awake.

Develop your time guesser

You perhaps notice some of your fellow salesmen are
better "time guessers" than others. An English salesman—
when awakened at any hour—can tell you the time within
three seconds of being absolutely correct. Some salesmen
train themselves to take, say, ten minutes for a coffee break.
At the end of ten minutes—without looking at the clock—
they're back at work. They have trained themselves to be
alert constantly to periods of time. This, of course, is one of
the top secrets of efficiency. Anyone can develop and apply
it—through faithful practice.

As children, we learn to count before we talk. Children born blind are sometimes the exception. That leads psychologists to believe that counting developed out of our early experience watching our fingers move. Some also believe our decimal system is based on this early experience of the race—and the fact that we have 10 fingers.

Our workaday concept of time is closely linked with counting: the year, month, week, day, hour, minute, second are all time counts. They depend on the waxing and waning of the moon, sunrise and sunset—upon our ability to devise calendars, clocks, speedometers, and the like. On them also depends the development of our time sense—in pacing our duties and commitments throughout the day.

Perhaps such time concepts as we've reviewed may make us more deferential to time. Perhaps they'll deepen our insight as we now count the hours and what we put into them. Perhaps they'll highlight how much time we have—if we but count it.

How to audit your 1,930 spare hours

By the way, did you know that you have 1,930 *spare* hours every single year? Maybe you don't think you have much spare time. Let's see. There are 365 days in a year, or 8,760 hours. Let us see how many of them are actually used.

Eight hours a night for sleep	2,920
Five workdays at eight hours a day for 49 weeks (allow 2 weeks vacation and seven holidays)	1,960
Two hours a working day to get to your first call and for paper work	490
Three hours a day (generous!) for meals	1,095
One hour a day for bathing, dressing, etc.	365
Total	6,830

Take 6,830 from 8,760 hours and you have 1,930 hours left to use as you see fit. This huge sum of time equals 80 days of 24 hours each—nearly 22 per cent of the year. It applies to most—but not all—of us.

The Royal Bank of Canada—in one of its excellent letters—recently pointed out that in 1850 the work week was 68 hours; now it is under 40. Your life expectancy grows greater too. So even more spare hours are ahead for you.

Look at your idle hours in terms of cash. What price do you put on your leisure? Five dollars an hour? If you do, your leisure hours are worth $9,650 a year! The fact that you are now committed to *professional* salesmanship, means you value your spare hours.

Harry J. Sheerin once remarked, "Time wasted is existence; used, it's life!" Let's use Harry Sheerin's thought to begin a check list—of ways to get more out of time.

Five ways to have enough time

1. *Plan your time.* Isn't this the secret of efficient self-management? With a plan you have enough time for any or all activities, such as:
Church attendance
Community responsibilities
Contemplation
Hobbies
More hours at work
More time with family
Participation in professional organizations
Self-improvement
Sports
A time plan is like a personal budget: some people can keep both without committing them to paper. Others have to draw up plans and refer to them constantly. Still others

begin with formal plans on paper. Once they discipline themselves that way, they can do without them—keep them mentally.

2. *Draw up a schedule and stick to it.* If you've never planned a schedule of your activities, you'll enjoy working one out. All you have to do is prepare a large sheet of paper with 7 vertical columns and 24 horizontal lines. You head the columns with the days of the week. Each of the 24 lines represents one hour. The column lines and hour lines form boxes. In these boxes write your planned activities. You can divide the boxes diagonally, if you want to schedule half-hours.

You may have to change your schedule from week to week. If you don't, so much the better. Once you've worked out a detailed schedule of your time, keep it before you. You may want to put it in a transparent folder. Refer to it throughout the day. Take it home with you. Make it part of your daily life.

Constantly evaluate your time allotments. For example, if you allow one hour for bathing and dressing, clock yourself. Keep to the schedule. Perhaps you can halve the time. Save that minute! Remember great things can be accomplished in spare minutes. Don't rush; cut out random movements.

3. *Increase your efficiency.* The salesman who trains himself to read 700 words a minute—instead of 350 words a minute—is saving 100 per cent of time whenever he reads.

Or consider two salesmen making retail calls in Manhattan. One averages 12 calls a day; the other 8 calls. The former achieved last year almost 90 per cent more sales than the latter—and remember, in the same time. How does he do it? By streamlining his presentations, principally.

A salesman friend for almost thirty-five years has carried a breakfast tray to his wife on Saturday, Sunday, holidays.

He says it's a wonderful investment. He prepares ordinarily a half grapefruit, bacon and eggs, toast and coffee. By breaking down "Operation Breakfast" into time-and-motion study, he now cooks breakfast in five minutes and two seconds! What's more, he says it's fun. He's the kind of fellow who makes a hobby of personal efficiency.

Thousands of ways to save time are within reach of everyone—if we have the drive to do it. Most salesmen feel the need to save time in:

Travel—finding shorter routes

Filling out reports

The presence of the buyer

Filing and record keeping

4. *Apply the economy-of-effort principle*. A definition of the economy-of-effort principle: "Never stand when you can sit; never sit when you can lie down." Salesman Sam boasts of his fast driving. He hits up to 80 miles an hour. Aside from the accident risk he takes, his record suffers. Because of his tenseness he makes a lot of mistakes. He also loses more days on account of illness than the average.

One day his manager noticed him driving on Roosevelt Boulevard in Philadelphia. Signs indicated the traffic lights were set for 30 mph steady driving. Salesman Sam drove 40 or more mph, waited for the red lights to change, shifted gears to a fast getaway—only to repeat the whole performance some fifteen times to the center of the city. His sales manager got there as quickly without stopping for one red light on the boulevard.

Ever notice a salesman talk so fast he has to repeat—rearrange his sentences? It's called "cluttering." If he were to slow down—speak more deliberately—he'd save himself time and energy. And his customers would understand him with less strain and confusion.

Through conscious control of the self, all of us can accomplish more with less effort. Such activities as sitting, getting up, eating, sleeping, walking, breathing, playing golf—all improve with the economy-of-effort principle. To expend only enough energy to get the desired result—this is a constant challenge. Faithfully applied, it prolongs life, deepens resourcefulness, and perks up efficiency. In short, it provides you with more time, health, and composure.

Any principle is hard to apply faithfully. Wasn't it Tolstoi who said, "It is easier to write ten books on philosophy than to apply one principle"? That holds for the economy-of-effort principle—particularly in our frenetic civilization. But it's well worth the effort—it pays such handsome returns.

5. *Love your work*. There's an old Chinese proverb— often attributed to Confucius. It goes like this:

> If you would be happy for one hour, take a nap.
> If you would be happy for a day, go fishing.
> If you would be happy for a week, kill your pig and eat it.
> If you would be happy for a month, get married.
> If you would be happy for a year, inherit a fortune.
> If you would be happy for life, love your work.

When a salesman loves his work, he crowds a lot of it into his 24 hours a day. He has the zest to become ever more efficient. He *makes* the time to get more things done. He eats better, sleeps better, lives longer. Through the work he loves, he finds an outlet for the great capacities bottled up within him. Frustrations and dejection he takes in stride. Nothing develops his time sense so keenly as love of work. And, incidentally, the salesman who is burning with love of work seldom gets fired!

7

How to Work Two Jobs at the Same Time

> Making a sale is not equivalent to creating a customer.
>
> FRED LAWRASON

The first job—customer keeping

The typical professional salesman has two jobs. Only when he works at both of them to produce maximum sales does he succeed.

He thinks of his first job as "maintenance selling." Here his goal is to keep his present customers and—if possible—increase the size of their orders. Because he's a strategist, he sees maintenance selling as a holding operation. (Competition doesn't make it easy.)

Yet it's the easier of his two jobs. For he knows the customers he has sold. He already has bonds with them—knows their needs, their personal quirks, their buying habits, and the like. If he's newly hired, ordinarily his company introduces him to its present customers in his territory. That way he maintains and strengthens relationships with customers.

82

Veteran salesmen have a favorite saying: "The best place to get more business is from present customers—people who've bought from you, have confidence in you and your firm. Help 'em sell more, and they'll buy more from you!" There's much wisdom in that saying. But the professional salesman isn't content to entrust his success to the present customers alone.

The other job—customer getting

He works equally hard—or harder—at his second job. He calls it "development selling." Here his goal is to create new customers. And this is more difficult to do. Result: The average salesman tends to neglect it. It's development selling that "separates the men from the boys."

MS vs DS

Let's review the main reasons why development selling (DS) is more difficult than maintenance selling (MS).

1. DS involves more rebuffs; MS entails more acceptance.

2. MS means calling on customers with whom you have already established friendly relations; DS requires you to make friends with customers who may not even want to see you.

3. DS requires you to identify and hunt out prospects. This means you have to locate the company first. Then you spend a lot of time learning the right man to call on. MS means calling on old accounts with your entree already established.

4. DS requires you to shape buyers' patterns of thought and attitudes—educate them about your products and services. This means you must get, understand, and use information about your buyers as individuals. You have to learn the needs and fears of each, how he thinks, his

likes and dislikes, his interests and ambitions. Then you must adapt this information as you work with him. In MS either this development work has already been done (by you or by someone else) or you're accepted as a reliable source of help and have access to those who make the buying decisions.

5. DS presents you with the challenge to change your prospect's buying habits and to support him psychologically as he goes through the changing process. In MS you have already brought these changes about.

6. DS demands more tact, better communication, more preparation of your sales presentations, greater command in answering objections, more follow-up than does MS.

In short, DS is so difficult that some large companies have recently made it a specialty. They select only gifted salesmen who do nothing else. These salesmen are the "chiefs"; those restricted to MS are often referred to as "Indians."

Because development selling makes so many demands upon the salesman, he who succeeds at it commands the highest rewards. However, the great majority of successful salesmen have to do both jobs and do them well. (They consider MS their bread and butter, DS their cake.) The secret of their success in both jobs begins with the way they manage their sales territory.

How to divide a territory

When Don Mitchell became head of Sylvania Electric Products, Inc., he called a sales meeting. He said, "Gentlemen, I've got good news for you!—We're going to divide your territories in half. . . ."

Faces fell. You heard suppressed groans here and there in the audience. For salesmen don't ordinarily like to see their territories shrunk. They think they won't be able to earn as much or their prestige will suffer.

But Don Mitchell went on. He said, "A year from today we're going to have our annual sales meeting. By then you're going to prove that you've sold as much, more, I predict, in your reduced territories." And they did just that. (Later, their territories were cut down in size again. Once more sales increased.)

Don Mitchell taught a most valuable lesson to Sylvania salesmen. This same lesson needs to be taught more widely. The reason many companies don't grow as they should is that their salesmen don't work their territories intensively enough. Why? Because they haven't been taught to organize their territories. Until each salesman organizes his territory, he can't make intelligent use of his selling time. And so profits slip through his and his company's fingers. You see, every unorganized sales territory has huge untapped potential. It's like a mother lode with rich veins running in all directions—waiting to be explored, assayed, mined.

As salesman, you're at once prospector, assayer, miner of your sales territory. It all takes planning. You can't work a territory hit or miss—if you want to get the most out of it.

Here's how

1. Adopt a winning attitude before you begin. Think of your sales territory as if it is your own company or business. See yourself as the president and general manager. Be as eager to make as much profit out of your territory as if you were your company's major stockholder. Then apply the principles of scientific sales management—and you'll reap huge rewards. Be careful if you do! You'll turn in such a stellar performance, you'll be promoted to heavier responsibility.

2. Fill out an account card for each of your customers
and prospects. Use 3- by 5-inch cards. Keep them in a jogger.
On each account card, write the name of one customer or
prospect. This may take you a good deal of time—especially
if you're new to the territory or if your predecessor left
no records for you. (Remember you have to find out who
your customers are in DS.) Moreover, this kind of record
keeping is a continuous chore. New customers and prospects move into your territory. Some move away. You'll
want to add information after each call. So keep your
account cards up to date.

3. Group your customers and prospects—your account
cards—by towns. Write the name of the town on a separate
index card. Alphabetize the account cards. Put them behind the index card for the appropriate town. Some salesmen attach an index clip to each town card—the name of
the town on the clip. This makes for quick reference.
Finally, group the towns by the counties, wards, or parishes
in which they're located. (If your territory is in a large city
or metropolitan area, group your customers and prospects
by wards, boroughs, sections, or other local divisions.)

4. Add basic information to each card. You have to decide—after studying your needs and company's policies—
what specifically to list on each account card. Here are
sample entries successful salesmen write on their account
cards:

The account's name, address, telephone number
Buyer's name and names of personnel you meet on your
   calls
The account's Dun & Bradstreet rating
Your company's limit of credit allowed the account
Purchases made by the account from your company
Buyer's birthday and chief interests

Ideas and services you've extended the buyer

Size and kind of order to propose on your next call

Now let's see where we are. By following the four steps, you've built a solid foundation. Your attitude's set for success. You have a quick, complete reference—and a detailed one—of your territory's sales potential. You have your accounts classified by towns, counties, or other geographical divisions. You have each account described and analyzed. You're now ready to proceed.

5. Prepare a work map of your entire territory. Often a road map—you can get one at a gasoline station—will do. If your sales territory is in a large city—get a city, borough, or ward map. (There are many companies that sell maps. Rand McNally & Co., 7 West 48th Street, New York City, is perhaps the largest. Sometimes stationery stores carry an assortment of maps, or they'll order one for you. *Sales Management*, 630 Third Avenue, New York City, recently published an article with two columns of companies that sell maps salesmen can use.)

Spread the map on a table top. Next to it put your jogger of 3- by 5-inch cards you've prepared—with your accounts arranged by towns or other divisions. Next to each town on the index cards, write the number of working hours you have to spend in each town and the number of visits you have to make each month. For example:

Middletown—4 hours, 2 times.

Now, locate the town on the map. Right next to it, write the information from the index cards. Use red pencil to indicate one call a month; blue, to indicate two calls a month; green, to indicate three calls a month. (Some salesmen get colored stars from a variety or stationery store. They paste them on the map instead of using colored pencils.)

Also on the map—next to the colored number—write the number of hours you have to spend in the town on every trip. For example:

Centerville—2 hours.

6. Prepare your weekly route maps. Here you work out the route you'll cover each week. Only when you prepare route maps can you reduce travel time, get rid of back-tracking and "merry-go-rounding," spend more time in the presence of the buyer, do more DS, make each work hour profitable.

Prepare one route map for each week in the month. This means at least four, sometimes five. The exact number you prepare depends on the frequency of your calls. You already have this information on your town cards.

Take a fresh map. Use an ordinary pencil—soft enough to erase well. Now, trace lightly the route you plan to follow the first week. The idea, of course, is to go by the shortest, quickest routes between towns.

Keep in mind the time it takes you to travel from your home to your first sales call, also the time you must spend in each town. Write O where you'll stop over night.

After you've traced your first week's route map, study it. Where can you save travel time? How early in the morning will you get up to cover the wide open spaces so you can make your first sales call at the earliest possible time?

When you're sure you have the most efficient travel route for your first week, trace it with ink.

Then proceed with the map for the second week—just as you did for the first week, and so on, until you've completed all your weekly route maps.

Once you do this, you may find you should move your residence—to the center of your sales territory. You can then think of your territory as a wheel. You live at the hub. Your weekly routes fan out from there as spokes in a wheel.

For example, let's recall the experience of the salesman, 85 per cent of whose customers were in or near Milwaukee, Wisconsin. The salesman lived 85 miles away at Menasha. There and in the surrounding towns were 35 per cent of his customers and prospects. Once he analyzed his territory, he discovered he sold almost the full potential of Menasha and the nearby towns, but only 50 per cent of his major market, Milwaukee. He and his family moved to a suburb of Milwaukee. Shortly after, his sales soared. He had organized his territory so that he spent more time selling, less time putting mileage on his speedometer. (Beware of the salesman who boasts of his annual mileage. Ask him what percentage of his potential is he selling?)

The basic reasons for your route maps are to provide you with a timesaving schedule, to multiply your selling hours, to distribute them among your vast sales opportunities.

One word more. If your map is large enough, you can put all four or five weeks of routes on it. When you do that, partition off each week's route in heavy crayon, using assorted colors.

7. Construct your weekly route lists. Your company may have forms for you to fill in your route lists. If not, use index cards or 8½- by 11-inch pages to be inserted in a ring binder.

Here you arrange your lists by days or half days. For example:

First Week:

    MON. A.M. West Carrolton, Franklin, Miamisburg (O) (Miamisburg Inn)

    TUES. A.M. Middletown, Hamilton

    TUES. P.M. Cincinnati (O) (Sinton Hotel)

    WED. A.M.–P.M. Cincinnati, etc.

Under each town, list your customers and prospects. List them in the order you plan to call on them, again from the standpoint of reducing travel and saving time. Don't hedge-hop all over town. Work it methodically.

8. Show your results to your supervisor or manager. Let him see your account cards, how you classify them by towns, the basic information you have on them, your work map, your weekly route map or maps, your weekly route lists. Ask him for his suggestions to improve upon what you've done. He'll admire you for the thoroughness of your procedures, for seeking his advice.

9. Give your supervisor or manager a copy of your weekly route lists. He'll then know how to reach you, particularly where you stay over night.

10. Keep a diary. In it write important matters you can't afford to trust to memory. You'll want to write in it promises to make call-backs, when to write letters and reports, when to attend meetings, store openings, conventions, and the like. Instead of a diary, some salesmen prefer to keep a separate set of cards—one for every day in the year. Take your choice.

11. Prepare a detailed schedule of DS for your territory. What per cent of your working time are you going to give it? So many hours each day? Or one day a week exclusively? Ask your supervisor or manager whether you are giving enough time to DS.

Seven benefits to you from organizing your territory

The steps to take in organizing your territory, you see, are simple. They involve only work. But bear in mind that by organizing your territory you:

1. Sell more
2. Render more service to your customers
3. Save time
4. Conserve your energy

5. Increase your DS
6. Develop habits of managing a territory that help to advance you
7. Give you the sense of achievement and growth

If you have never done so, you'll probably gain much from asking a straight commission salesman, "Mind telling me how you organize your territory?" You'll probably get from him the impression that he spends a lot of time on organizing his territory—a lot of time also on his records and paper work. Do you know why he does so? Not because he particularly enjoys the process. But because he's learned that he can earn big money only by making the most and best use of his time.

Seven major weaknesses

Recently, a life insurance company queried sales managers on the major weaknesses of salesmen. The seven most often-mentioned weaknesses:

1. Failure to utilize time in work
2. Failure to organize work
3. Failure to plan work
4. Failure to use enough selling time
5. Failure to have enough product information
6. Failure to use enough effort
7. Failure in prospecting for new business

How many of these seven weaknesses would disappear—if salesmen would organize (and work) their territories as you have just planned?

Someone has said that the young salesman who organizes his territory—and works it economically—fulfills the adage that "an old young man will be a young old man."

8

How to Listen to Customers with Your Third Ear

> Man has two ears and one tongue that he may listen twice as much as he speaks.
>
> EPICTETUS

Dr. Carl R. Rogers, eminent psychologist, has made an excellent contribution to salesmen—and all others who want to learn to listen intelligently. In his counseling, Dr. Rogers finds the best way to get in rapport with the speaker is to reflect his feelings.

Once salesmen learn to do this, they make more sales. They know that listening is much more than just hearing or interpreting words. It is, at its best, tuning in to the other fellow's feelings and frame of mind—showing him you sympathize.

Five ways to tune in on feelings

The best way to tune in to the other fellow's feelings is to reflect them as he talks. Just how do you do this?

1. Look at him sympathetically.

2. Keep quiet while he talks—don't interrupt, except to give a word or two of reassurance.

3. Don't impose your will upon him.

4. Don't argue with him.

5. Don't make him feel guilty.

As you reflect his feelings and echo them, you do two things. In the first place, you give him confidence in you as a sympathetic, understanding person. Emerson touched the skirts of this same situation: "When you share a sorrow, it lessens. When you share a joy, it increases."

In the second place, you actually give him more insight. How often in the presence of a sympathetic listener does the speaker work out his problem—simply by putting it into words. As he talks he rejects some ideas, endorses others —rearranges them and finds a solution.

Helping the buyer pick up the pieces

Let's take an example: Suppose you approach a buyer who's obviously distressed. You notice that he looks worried. You don't see his usual smile. He looks rather pale and drawn. The conversation goes like this:

SALESMAN: Good afternoon, Mr. Smith, how's business?

BUYER: Terrible—maybe you'd better drop by another time.

SALESMAN: Oh, I'm sorry. Isn't there something I can do to
• help?

BUYER: No. The bookkeeper left town—took all my records— The business is in a mess. They think he stole a lot of money too.

SALESMAN: Well that's too bad. I'm so sorry.

BUYER: Yeah, I never did have faith in that fellow. They should've been wise to him—driving that expensive car and living high on the hog; and on his salary too!

SALESMAN: Well, it's one of those things. Happens every day somewhere, doesn't it?

BUYER: Gee, hadn't thought of that too much.

SALESMAN: Yes, there's usually a way out, isn't there?

BUYER: Yeah, but damned if I know where to start, what with all I've got to do. Well, I guess you've got to start somewhere.

SALESMAN: That's for sure! Would a salesman's records help?

BUYER: By the way, have you got the records of our recent sales? How far back do yours go?

SALESMAN: Why, let's see—I've got those from my last visit—copies of all the others in my files at home.

BUYER: Well that'll help some. When can I get 'em?

SALESMAN: How's day after tomorrow?

BUYER: Would you? That's O.K. Say, you know what? I'm going to get in touch with all the others I buy from. At least the old man'll know the Purchasing Department is on the ball!

Now, do you see how you can apply Dr. Rogers's technique in the presence of the buyer? By reflecting the buyer's feelings, the salesman got him to share his worry. The salesman also got the buyer to understand his own feelings—led him, thereby, to do something constructive.

The salesman did this by showing a deep interest in what the buyer had to say. He agreed with him. (Disraeli used to say an agreeable person is one who agrees with you.) Notice that the salesman didn't overwhelm the buyer with talk—didn't curse the runaway bookkeeper. Rather, he trod the soft pedal—just said enough to let the buyer know he was listening sympathetically.

The salesman repeated the buyer's sentiments—didn't disapprove of them. He also guided the buyer into doing something other than stew about his problem. But how tactfully he did it! He didn't force him by logic or direct appeal.

Why not reread the dialogue at this point? It actually happened.

The nondirective approach

Here's another way to listen with your third ear. It's closely related to Dr. Rogers's approach. Personnel specialists call it "the nondirective interview." It's particularly useful when you want to drain off tensions caused by complaints and worries. All you have to do is listen sympathetically without butting in.

Just before Gen. George C. Marshall sent Gen. H. H. ("Hap") Arnold to the Southwest Pacific in 1942 he said to him: "I'd like to make three suggestions about carrying out your responsibilities of leadership out there: (1) Listen to the other fellow's story; (2) don't get mad; (3) let the other fellow tell his story first."

General Marshall gave General Arnold an excellent working definition of the nondirective interview. He also gave him sound advice. Using it, General Arnold became one of the most popular and accomplished leaders of World War II.

You can use the same approach, particularly when you listen to customer complaints. Many salesmen build ill will and lose orders simply because they don't know how to listen to complaints.

Anatomy of a complaint

For one thing, they don't always understand the anatomy of a complaint. A complaint is based on real or imaginary injury. Often it springs from something trivial—at a time when the buyer has a stomach-ache or a raft of problems, or maybe he had a tiff with his wife at breakfast. His frustration tolerance is low. Just on this day the salesman pokes his head in the door. And "Pow!"—all the buyer's aches and worries are aimed at the poor salesman, whether he (or his company) is to blame or not.

If, at this crucial moment, the salesman argues or tries to reason with the irate buyer, all is likely to be lost. But if the salesman suggests to *himself,* "Oh, he isn't as tough as he looks or sounds! Let's play with him for a bit until he gets done thrashing around—then we'll land him!"—then the salesman understands and wins the first round.

He wins the second round when he reveals a readiness to hear the buyer out, speaking as little as possible. (Who was it who said, "The best way of answering a bad argument is to let it go on"?)

This too is hard to do. Your natural reaction is to strike back—to defend yourself and your company, to have your say, to put him right, to tell him off.

But now that you understand the nondirective approach, you'll let him spout off. As he does so, you'll reflect your regret in your face and manner. Just about all you'll say will be something like "I'm sorry, Mr. Jones." Perhaps he'll erupt further. But notice his second explosion will ordinarily have less fireworks than the first. He's getting it off his chest. You may even want to purge his spleen further with "There's obviously a misunderstanding, Mr. Jones. I want very much to hear your side of the story."

Now he may be off to the races again. Don't interrupt him. Before long—if you've maintained your deferential listening—he'll begin to quiet down, will start feeling guilty because he's treated you shabbily. And you've not tried to get even. "A soft answer turneth away wrath," the Bible says. And you've demonstrated it.

Traditionally, Japanese youngsters are trained to smile and bow while a parent or teacher berates them. They're taught this early in life to good advantage later on—when they have to work for a hard boss, for instance. You won't want to do that—smile and scrape—when the storm breaks. But you'll find deferential listening a great boon to your salesmanship.

Seven ways to improve your listening ability

Here are some other things professional salesmen know about listening:

1. *Analyze the buyer's temperament.* Don't react to his words only. Decide what kind of a person he is. This takes time and acquaintance. For men, like melons, are hard to know. Suppose, for example, he's a worrywart. He says to you, "That new item of yours won't go over!" His remark means something quite different from the same words spoken by an optimist. The worrywart needs more reassurance than the optimist. Until you understand the buyer's basic temperament, you can't listen intelligently to him.

Therefore, identify your buyers by their habitual way of looking at life. You'll find some pessimists; others optimists; still others alarmists; some others unpredictable. They may be one way today, another tomorrow. Govern your listening and responses to them by two basic questions:

How and what does he feel?

What does he mean by what he says?

2. *Listen beyond his words—for their intent.* A buyer with a sarcastic way of speaking was unpopular with two successive salesmen—from the same company. (Both quit.) A characteristic remark of the buyer was "You salesmen are a big nuisance. Wish you'd get lost. You take too much of my time. I could do better ordering from a catalogue." A third salesman didn't take the buyer's words at their face value. He wasn't hurt by them. He played along with the buyer. He'd reply, "How right you are, Mr. Jones! But gosh, that wife of mine eats like a bird—a vulture! And

you've just got to help me feed her." That salesman got along very well with the buyer. He knew the buyer didn't really mean his words to be interpreted literally.

In Owen Wister's great story *The Virginian*, the leading character's famous remark—"Smile when you call me that!" —is very much to the point. The words themselves often count less than the intent behind them. The professional salesman is therefore alert to intent first.

3. *Make sure of the meaning of his words.* A salesman of engine preheaters persuaded a gasoline station operator to buy some shares of his company's *stock*. The operator also ordered a gross of heaters—a rather large inventory for him. It was during a labor shortage when he couldn't get mechanics to install the heaters. The salesman called to ask the operator to pay for his order. The operator said he hadn't sold any. The salesman then asked him to return the stock. The operator wrote the company and protested. He wanted to retain his stock in the company. But he requested permission to return his inventory. The salesman had used "stock" in the sense of "inventory," which the operator misinterpreted.

How often—especially in the course of sales presentations interrupted in the hurry of conducting business— does the salesman (or the customer) misinterpret words! He doesn't listen analytically enough.

A salesman congratulated a buyer on his daughter's engagement. Here's their chat:

BUYER: Thank you. Last night her friends gave her a shower. You should've seen the presents!
SALESMAN: That's nice. I hope she got a good haul.
BUYER: Oh, yes! He's a very nice fellow.

Later on the salesman realized that the buyer misinterpreted "haul." The salesman referred, of course, to the presents.

4. *Don't indulge in wishful listening.* A pharmaceutical salesman made a survey within his own territory of hospital sales. (His company sold to hospitals through a distributor.) The salesman recommended that he call on hospitals in his own territory as well as his own customers—druggists. His sales manager congratulated him on his aggressiveness: "Keep up the good work! Maybe some day we'll have our own sales force to service the hospitals—and you'll be in on the ground floor."

Shortly after, the salesman wrote his manager, "My wife and I are happy that the company is going to set up a separate sales division for hospitals and I'll be considered to head it up."

The sales manager became angry. He resented the salesman's reading too much into his remarks. He gave the salesman a lecture on wishful listening.

Another example: A buyer said to a salesman, "*Sometime* when we open a new supermarket, I'll let you conduct a store sale." Next time the grocery chain announced an opening, the salesman was on hand early in the morning. He asked the store manager where he could build a point-of-purchase display to hold his store sale. The manager said he had no room for him. This all led to a call to the buyer. He pointed out that he had made a casual remark—that the salesman was trying to twist his arm. Actually the salesman was sincere in his belief that he had had a commitment. He had let his ears hear his hopes rather than the buyer's intent.

Be careful to check your understanding of what you hear. One good way to do this is to repeat the idea in your own words: "Do I understand you right that when and if we have a hospital sales division I may be considered to head it up?" Or, "Thank you. Does that mean that I may hold a store sale at your *next* opening? May I phone you to confirm it?"

5. *Increase your auditory memory span.* With practice you can train yourself to repeat 10 or more digits immediately after you hear them, for example, 6–8–1–9–3–7–4–2–5–1.

The way to do this is to have some one call out numbers of increasing length and after the end of each say "Write." Then you write as many of the digits as you recall. For example:

7–3–8–2
9–7–2–5–3
1–8–2–7–6–9
2–4–7–8–6–1–3
7–1–9–6–2–8–3–6
3–9–2–8–5–4–6–7–1

Score your results. Do this exercise every evening for ten minutes—change the numbers each time—for a month. You'll be amazed at the growth in your auditory memory span.

Likewise, you can increase your auditory memory span for words and sentences. Here's how: Have someone read short paragraphs to you in phrases—pausing at logical places. After the reading have him (or her) say "Write." Then write what you have heard with as many of the original words as you recall. For example (the vertical lines indicate pauses):

a. When psychologists use the terms / introvert and extrovert / to classify people / according to personality / they don't mean / anybody is completely / one or the other./

b. A lot of people argue / that there was more joy in marriage / in the good old days./ To prove their point / they cite the fact / that divorce used to be a rare exception./ But they forget / that divorce / had to be an exception / in those days / because the weight of convention / was against it./ What was the use / of ending / a miserable marriage / when the criticism / that followed / was even worse?/

c. When it comes to neckties / salesmen have a real chance / to express their individuality./ Experts say / the more daring ties / should be left to men / with dynamic personalities./ Males with dark hair and eyes / may also take a fling at them./ Striped ties are dangerous / with a striped suit and shirt./ Yellow and orange ties / increase an already sallow complexion./ Bow ties / make a face broader./ And fantastic hand-painted ties / can be frightful / unless the wearer's personality / is distinctly / on the jaunty side./ Ties can include everything / from an old-school stripe / to a picture / of a bubble dancer./ The latter of course / is inadvisable / especially when calling on a customer./

Have your helper read slowly. Correct what you write—after each reading. Use different paragraphs each evening. Notice how your increased auditory span serves you well in listening to your customers.

6. *Take care of your hearing.* If you suspect your hearing is dull, get an audiometric test. Get in touch with an ear specialist or your local League for the Hard of Hearing. There you can probably get a hearing test and advice. You need good hearing—with or without a mechanical aid—to listen well.

7. *Check up now and then on your listening skill.* Answer the following questions. You'll then be sure to touch all bases.

a. Is my hearing acute enough to listen well?

b. Is my sight keen enough to interpret the buyer's facial expressions?

c. Do I sit or stand in the presence of the buyer so as to see his face as he talks?

d. Do I understand his words as he intends them?

e. Do I weigh the buyer's words, thoughts, questions, objections from his point of view?

f. Do I restate accurately in my own mind the ideas and feelings the buyer conveys?

g. Do I repeat to the buyer—if necessary—in my own words the idea he expresses?

h. Do I avoid misunderstanding by being specific?

i. Do I search for the meaning of his words and what's behind them?

j. Am I on the lookout for opinions and facts and do I not confuse the two?

k. Do I pinpoint assumptions in the buyer's talk and help him see the facts clearly?

l. Do I listen for the source of his information—whether it is experience, observation, somebody else's opinion?

m. Do I study the buyer's voice, posture, actions, facial expressions—as he talks?

n. Do I give him plenty of opportunity to talk?

o. Do I evaluate *how* the buyer says things because how he says them often tells more than *what* he says?

p. Do I avoid wishful listening?

q. Do I review my successful and unsuccessful sales presentations—to analyze the part listening played in them?

r. Do I listen past the "no's," refusals, and excuses for not buying—for their real meaning?

s. Do I use listening as a means of draining off the buyer's emotional resistance?

t. Do I agree with Epictetus that "nature has given to men one tongue, but two ears, that we may hear from others twice as much as we speak"?

9

How to Use 11 Different Kinds of Questions in Making Your Sales Presentation

The man who can't ask, can't learn.

PROVERB

Have you ever heard the delightful story of the two monks? One was a young monk, the other, quite old. It was their pleasant custom to read their prayers at eventide in the garden of their monastery.

One evening the young monk noticed the old monk smoking his pipe while he read his breviary. The young monk hurried over and said, "Why, Father! I'm amazed to see you smoke while you pray!—When I entered the monastery I asked the abbot, 'Father, is it all right if I smoke while I pray?' "

" 'Of course not, my son,' " he answered, " 'I'm surprised you even asked!' "

"Well now," said the old monk, "you didn't ask him right! You see, Father, years ago I asked the Reverend Abbot the same question—but in a slightly different way.

103

Am I correct? You asked him, 'Is it all right if I smoke while I pray?' "

"That's right," replied the young monk.

"Well, Father," said the old monk with a twinkle in his eye, "I put it to him this way: 'Reverend Father, is it all right if I pray while I smoke?' "

" 'Why of course, my son,' said the abbot as he gave me his benediction! 'That's an excellent idea!' "

Ten benefits of the art of asking questions

As you well know, there's an art to asking questions. Professional salesmen master this art. They listen, classify, and practice using questions. They analyze the question technique of excellent conversationalists, interviewers, lawyers—and salesmen. This art—once mastered and faithfully used—is a powerful sales aid. It's worth your deepest study, constant use, regular evaluation. For when you ask questions skillfully in your sales interviews, you accomplish many things:

1. You can acquire needed information.
2. You can uncover objections that the reticent buyer may not otherwise share with you.
3. By doing this, you can meet his objections.
4. You can make sure he's listening to you.
5. You can also make sure he's understanding you as you intend.
6. You can get him to agree with you—to put him in receptive mind for the order you'll suggest.
7. You can encourage him to participate in the sales presentation—thus make it a pleasing two-way activity rather than a "lecture."
8. You can discover what motives interest him most.
9. You can help him to make the decision to buy.
10. You can build rapport with your buyer.

You can accomplish these 10 goals—as needed—by learning the different types of questions and by applying them when you prepare and deliver your sales presentations.

Kinds of questions professional salesmen use

Let's take up 11 different kinds of questions that successful salesmen use every day. They use them by design at various stages of the sales interview—to gain their objectives. By doing so, they prove themselves masterful psychologists.

1. *The direct.* You may recall Kipling's couplet:

> I have six serving-men
> (They taught me all I know)
> Their names are What and Why and When
> And How and Where and Who.

What, why, when, how, where, who are keys to direct questions. For example:

a. What price is your competitor getting?
b. Why didn't you let me know about the damaged merchandise?
c. When did you place the ad?
d. How many shipments did you receive last month?
e. Where shall I set up the display?
f. Who should get credit for the promotion?

They tell us the average American boy of four asks 400 questions a day. We know how annoying his questions can be—yet how much he learns by asking them. We sometimes resent his question avalanche because (a) his questions give him a kind of dominance over us; (b) so many of them seem self-centered or senseless; (c) they sometimes expose our ignorance and build frustration; (d) some of them are too personal.

The buyer likewise often resents direct questions, especially if (a) they're too numerous; (b) they're too prying (personal); (c) they make him feel subservient; (d) they make him feel inferior; (e) they're too abrupt. Therefore, direct questions that alienate the buyer are blocks to getting the order.

So keep the buyer's point of view in mind when you ask him direct questions. To show him deference, you can begin your direct question with "May I ask, what. . . ?" Also, you can take the sharp edge off if you use his name: "Mr. Smith, how would you. . . ?" When you have to ask him a series of direct questions, point out benefits to accrue to him from his answers: "Mr. Smith, to help you select the best securities for *you,* may I first ask you several basic questions?"

When you ask direct questions in such gracious ways, you get more cooperation and fuller answers.

2. *The indirect.* Often you can get information more deftly with an indirect question. Instead of asking "What profit margin are you working on?" you put the question indirectly: "If we knew what profit margin your company is working on . . . ?"

Ordinarily your indirect question will get you as much information as the direct sort—or more. However, when it doesn't work, you can follow through with a direct question. In that event you may want to defer the direct question for a minute. Return to it after you've diverted the buyer's attention. Don't crowd him.

3. *The lead.* On the surface the lead resembles the indirect question. They differ not so much in form as purpose. When you ask, "I wonder, Mr. Smith, whether you too believe all businesses these days have to make innovations . . . ?" your intent is to get him to reveal an attitude —to encourage him to talk, not to get specific information.

Your lead questions, therefore, are "open enders"—designed to "feel him out." That way you can determine what motives to use in getting him to buy. As he talks, you estimate whether *convenience, gain, pride, security*—or a combination of these—will appeal to him most. Once you decide, you can then proceed with a tailor-made approach.

4. *The confirmation.* You use it to get your buyer to agree with you. "Am I right, Mr. Smith, that you're interested in maintaining the quality of your products, yet you want to buy them at a lower price?" "Weren't you pleased, Mr. Jones, with the unexpected rebate?" Sometimes all you have to say is, "Right?" or "O.K.?" (They're good questions to hold his attention too.)

The answer to a confirming question binds the buyer to you. Your question and his answer form a kind of contract between you. Since you know ahead of time what his answer will be—you have a powerful advantage.

The acid test of a good confirming question is a predictable "yes" or "no" answer. Therefore, make sure your confirming question will get the desired answer before you ask it.

5. *The feedback.* When you want to help the buyer crystallize his thinking—when you want him to confirm or even restate it—you "feed back" to him something he has already said. And you put it in the form of a question. For example, suppose an insurance investment salesman says to a young couple, "Now as I understand it, Mr. and Mrs. Jones, your main concern is to assure Junior enough funds for a college education?" Here the salesman has isolated the buyers' interest; got the couple to focus their interest; used, to good effect, something they had said; provided himself with a definite sales target. From then on he builds his presentation accordingly.

The feedback question usually begets a "Yes," "No,"

"That's right," "Not exactly," or another such response— as in the case of the confirming question. But notice that its purpose is different. If the buyer should deny something he has said, don't argue with him. Try another feedback or some other approach.

6. *The swivel.* Here you have a technique to help your buyer make a choice—come to a decision. You present him with alternatives: "Which color of these three sedans do you like best, Mr. White?"

One chain drugstore reported a 250 per cent increase in the sale of eggs at its lunch counters. The counter men were taught to ask customers ordering milk shakes or malted milks, "Will you have one or two farm-fresh eggs in it?" Most of the customers never had eggs in their milk shakes before—never thought of having them. Yet a large percentage answered "One." Virtually none of them said "Two."

You can use the swivel in other ways too. Suppose a buyer hasn't heard of your company—mentions that he's satisfied to stay with a present supplier, a big-name company:

SALESMAN: I can appreciate your point, Mr. Murphy. But may I ask, which would you prefer: a small, growing company —that's eager to extend tailor-made services and excellent products to its expanding clientele—or a large company that has to mass-produce its services and treat all its customers alike?

Or the objection may be: "But your line costs more."

SALESMAN: That's right, Mr. Morris. But which would you like better, a quality line—that gives your customers more satisfaction and you a higher markup—or a run-of-the-mill line?

Do you see the immense possibilities of persuasion in the swivel?

7. *The challenge.* There's a strong negative streak in many of us. When someone says we can't do so and so, our impulse is to show him he's wrong—to challenge him. The keen salesman discovers this tendency among some of his buyers; turns it to his advantage with the challenge.

A salesman who has led his division for years calls on supermarket chains—corporate and independent. He uses the challenging question with some buyers in both types of chains; finds the independent chain buyers especially susceptible to it.

An example of his use of a challenging question with a buyer of an independent chain:

SALESMAN: Mr. Black, this promotion went over with a bang with my largest corporate chain customer. But frankly there's a question in my mind, would it go over with a smaller, an independent, chain?

Then he sometimes uses a similar approach with the buyer of a corporate chain:

SALESMAN: This up-and-coming competitor of yours, Mr. Green, the local four-store chain, had a phenomenal success with this promotion. But frankly, I wonder whether we could get needed cooperation from your regional office to make it go with your markets?

A coal salesman had a premium offer. If a dealer ordered two cars of egg-sized anthracite he could have a Deepfreeze or TV set without cost. In approaching smaller dealers, one salesman had much success with this approach:

SALESMAN: It's too bad your yard has so many partitions, Mr. Gray. You can't take advantage of this wonderful offer. Your wife would love the premium. But we couldn't ask you to remove a partition in your yard to accommodate two cars of "egg," could we?

If you know your buyer well enough to decide he's negatively disposed, you'll want to try an occasional challenge on him. If you present it skillfully, he'll rise to bait just to show you!

8. *The silent.* Merely a raised eyebrow sometimes is more potent than a phrased question. It works well, ordinarily, when you need to doubt something your buyer has just said. You don't want to contradict him in words, so you furrow your brow instead. This may urge him to qualify or amplify his statement. Or suppose he doesn't answer your direct or indirect question. Express expectancy in your facial tensions and wait. He'll likely follow through.

As you may know, babies learn to interpret facial expressions long before they understand words. This fact is very valuable to remember for this reason. There's a psychological law that states that the things we learn earliest are the easiest to arouse. Therefore, you'll want to make much use of facial expression in your selling. Use it as a supplement to your words—as a substitute at times for speech, as in the instance of the silent question.

But don't grimace or overdo facial expressions. Why not practice them before a mirror? Why not begin with expressing doubt or expectancy? Then apply your skill on your sales calls. And remember—just because facial expressions are so powerful—you'll use them with the same care as you select your words. You can call a buyer a liar just as neatly with an eyebrow as a tongue.

9. *The assumption.* Great salesmen transfer the air of plausibility to their prospects and buyers. One of the ways they do this is with the assumptive question. For example:

SALESMAN (to a receptionist): Would you like to help me?—I don't know who in your organization is the best one to see about . . .

SALESMAN (to customer): Of course, Mr. Jones, since you've just installed gas heat in your home you'll want to have the best insulation, won't you? (That's why you'll find these storm windows such great money savers.)

Remember, most people find it easier to agree than disagree—especially when you aim a suggestion at their welfare or superiority. When you ask someone for help, you ordinarily pay him an implied compliment—to his high position, greater competence, or wisdom.

You can also use the assumption to save a buyer's face. Suppose a friendly buyer shows you a list of his needs. You spot an obvious mistake. Instead of saying, "John, haven't you made a mistake?" you may want to say, "Would you have time to let me read the list back to you as I write it in my order book?"

Your assumptive questions, you'll find, are among the most pleasant and useful of all you use.

10. *The stimulator.* Here your objective is to get the buyer to think to your advantage. Suppose the buyer resists taking your line because he has a competitive line in a different price range.

SALESMAN: You know, Mr. McDermott, you can't sell from an empty showcase. Have you ever thought, may I ask, how much business you lose because you don't carry the full price range?

Suppose that you are trying to sell a set of encyclopedias to a doubtful parent.

SALESMAN: You say, Mrs. Terrill, that your children are passing all their subjects in school. That's fine! Congratulations! But have you considered, Mrs. Terrill, that once they have our excellent children's encyclopedia they can do even better—get a lot of A's?

Or perhaps you are trying to convince a buyer that he should try your line of printing paper.

SALESMAN: How much saving, Mr. Eastham, would you say this new printing paper would save you on an average run?

Even though the stimulator may not always lead to an order, it very often does. Moreover, you can use it to get the buyer's attention and reactions. Salesmanship is a tug of minds, and the stimulator helps you pull the buyer's thoughts in your direction—gets his attention and reactions—anticipates his objections.

11. *The milestone.* In a sustained sales presentation you may cover many advantages and benefits of your products or services. Your buyer may accept some, reject others. As you proceed, you sort out the acceptances from the rejections. You restate those he's accepted. One of the best ways to do this is with the milestone question.

Let's listen to a paper salesman who'd like to sell the buyer his full line of consumer products. These include table napkins, cocktail napkins, facial tissues, paper cups, and toilet tissue.

SALESMAN: Am I right, Mr. Young, you're satisfied with your present line of toilet tissue but you're interested in taking on a line of paper cups and cocktail napkins?

BUYER: That's right.

SALESMAN: That's fine. Incidentally, you've selected the two items with the highest markup for you. Now, if I could show you a special tie-in deal—with 25 cents a case more profit on table napkins than you're now making—would you be interested?

BUYER: I might.

Notice how the salesman summarizes the buyer's decisions at two stages of his sales presentation. Now, let's continue with the conclusion of his presentation.

SALESMAN: Thank you, Mr. Young, for giving me so much time. Now, may I have just one more minute? Here is your order: 10 cases of cocktail napkins and the tie-in of 5 cases of table napkins, 20 cases of paper cups. Then, you know, you said you'd like me to help you move the merchandise in a store sale. How will next Tuesday suit your convenience? I'll be in Monday afternoon late—is that convenient?—to set up the display. I predict you'll be so pleased with the results, Mr. Young, you'll want our full line. Thank you very much.

Did you know that some buyers report that more than 50 per cent of all salesmen don't ask for the order? Of all the milestone questions this one is the most important.

Don't forget to ask for the order!

Five benefits of questions

In summary then, remember:

1. Questions are powerful sales tools.

2. They have many uses other than to get information.

3. They help you estimate attitudes, uncover objections, get reactions, enlist participation.

4. Questions are excellent substitutes for high-pressure, arm-twisting salesmanship. They provide amenities. Used wisely, questions up the salesman's popularity with his customers.

5. Questions help you streamline and pace your sales presentations.

Assignment

Write out 10 or more questions described in this chapter. Let them be questions you can use in your sales presentations. Practice them before a mirror and, if possible, record them and play them back. Use them and their like in your sales presentations. And notice the growth in your sales.

10

How to Develop and Deliver a Creative Sales Presentation

> The shrewd guess, the fertile hypothesis, the courageous leap to a tentative conclusion—these are the most valuable coin of the thinker at work, whatever his line of work.
>
> J. S. BRUNER

Generalship

Like the successful general, you—as a professional salesman—are a strategist and tactician. You plan your moves. You have alternatives for emergencies. You don't rely on sudden inspiration or divine intervention to win the battle or get the order—even though these may work for you on occasion. Rather, you study your buyer or customer, his needs, his motives for buying, how you—rather than your competitors—can best meet his needs.

And like the general too, you spend most of your work hours planning. Did you know that many high-level salesmen average only one hour a day in the presence of the buyer? Planning, travel, waiting take up the other eight or ten hours of their workday. This makes direct selling time valuable indeed. Now, to make the hour count, you have to fill it with orders. The best way to do this is to plan and deliver your sales presentation on a sound psychological basis.

Accent psychology

This is interesting, if not easy, to do because psychology challenges the professional salesman on several counts. In the first place, he's likely to be introspective. While his customers may think of him as an uncomplicated, outgoing personality—actually he's a bundle of keen sensibilities. He has as many feelings of inferiority as the average man, if not more. He indulges in a lot of self-analysis. He subscribes to something Socrates said, "The unexamined life is the worthless life." His study of his own actions and reactions makes him a devotee of psychology.

In the second place, he realizes his customers aren't always what they seem to be either. Their real motives for buying—or refusing to buy—may be deep-seated, involved, unrecognized by themselves. Psychology helps him to appreciate—and make use of—the hidden, complicated, enigmatic motives of his customers.

In the third place, he knows psychology grows steadily as a science. He wants to keep abreast of its major discoveries. Through his study he finds new answers to old problems—involving attention, rapport, desires, speech, creativity, etc. On the daily firing line, he's particularly concerned with the question: How can I make my sales presentations influence the mind and emotions of my customers to buy from me? His ability to deal with that question measures his sales success. And psychology holds the answer.

Psychology of motivation

The professional salesman's study of psychology—
through direct experience and study—leads him early in
his career to a definite conclusion: Mere appeal to the customer's conscious mind—to nis reason and common sense
—isn't always enough to get the order. The "logician's"
presentation in Chapter 17 exemplifies how all the reasons
why the dealer *should* buy didn't sell him. If salesmanship
were based solely on appeal to reason, salesmen wouldn't
have so much hard work to do.

He knows too that subconscious motives—largely emotional in nature—lie buried in the customer's past. They
are a bewildering mixture of unreasonable likes and dislikes, repressions, conflicts, hidden personal values, daydreams, unconscious attitudes, and the like—evolving since
infancy. Moreover—like the classic analogy of the iceberg,
at least 90 per cent of whose mass is below surface—their
potential outweighs that of conscious motives. The latter
you can compare to the 10 per cent of the iceberg that's
visible.

Ray C. Brewster, well-known sales executive, uses another comparison to explain the conscious and the subconscious mind. He says: "We might compare the two parts
of the mind with a watch. The face is like the conscious
mind, while the works represent the subconscious; the
conscious mind tells the time, the subconscious supplies
the wherewithal." The professional salesman is attentive
to both face and works.

What to do

Subconscious motives are highly involved. They even
bewilder psychiatrists and psychoanalysts sometimes. What

then can the salesman do about them—particularly those in the mind of the buyer?

Surveys of professional salesmen uncover two hints. They mention them oftener than any others: (1) As you prepare and deliver your ideas feel yourself constantly into the customer's point of view; (2) be a likable and not a domineering person. These two hints pretty well define low-pressure selling. Edward C. Bursk some years ago pointed out in *Harvard Business Review* that salesmanship is "closely related to the bewildering variousness of human nature—and this again is one reason why low-pressure selling, with its flexibility and adaptability, is both effective and more fun."

Notice, the two hints don't exempt the salesman from presenting the customers with ideas persuasively. It isn't enough for a salesman just to be a likable person. Recently a salesman—popular with his buyers—was retired three years early because he couldn't compete. Three of his buyers—they hadn't bought from him for two years—organized a testimonial dinner for him. They liked him enormously as a conversationalist, luncheon companion, friend. But they bought from his idea-giving competitors. Of course, the professional salesman must be likable, but he must also help his customers buy. He must help his buyers sell too. It's the combination of the two that gets the orders.

Anatomy of LPS

LPS (low-pressure selling), therefore, is psychologically sound. It's rooted in integrity, as it represents the customer's interest and welfare. It's aimed at the customer's dignity—at his right to accept or reject—without the effrontery of high-pressure argument. To quote Ray C. Brewster:

Man instinctively clings to certain dignities which endow his life with little personal glories. He is proud of the dignity of his birth, no matter how humble. He loves the dignity of personal superiority—and, above all, nothing is more precious than the dignity of making his own decisions—particularly decisions to buy. Unless the prospect instinctively feels that his contemplated decision to buy is sound, voluntary, and in line with his own best interests, it will not "pass" in his conscious mind—even if the need or want is fairly substantial.

The professional salesman remembers this constantly—whether he's planning a presentation or delivering it. It's his surest way to influence the subconscious as well as the conscious mind of the customer.

The creative sales presentation

The professional sales presentation is an adventure in creativity. It's a distinct type of speech, illustrated. It's creative because the salesman tailors it to the specific needs of a specific customer. It presupposes:

1. Thorough knowledge of the product or service you're selling
2. Analysis of the buyer and his needs
3. Ability to prepare, if necessary, a personalized visual aid to use in the presentation
4. Skill in making the presentation—to help the buyer realize his needs
5. Capacity to meet the buyer's needs to his satisfaction

When you prepare your sales presentation in a masterly way and rehearse it, your delivery of it has all the felicity of artlessness. It then seems spontaneous and improvised. And that's just the impression you want to create. For the perfection of art is to conceal art. And this too is good psychology.

Swap ideas for orders

Lionel B. Moses, vice-president of Parade Publications, Inc., tells a story about a young salesman and a gray-whiskered owner of a general store in the Pacific Northwest. The old man asked the inexperienced salesman, "What's new?"

The question hadn't come up in the training school, so naturally the young man was nonplused. He stammered and came out with a comment about the World Series.

"I'm not talking about that sort of thing," said the store-keeper. Then he went on, "Excuse me, young fellow, you haven't been here before, have you? I didn't notice that you were a new one," he exclaimed, "so I thought you would know what I meant. I've got a rule. All the salesmen who call on me know it. The rule is that if you give me an idea that I can use in my business, I give you an order you can use in your business. The idea can be on your products, or on something that has no connection with your products; I don't care. But I don't give orders; I swap orders for ideas!"

This stymied the young salesman. He later reported, "I couldn't have dug up an idea if my life depended on it." (He didn't get the order.)

"It was a month later when I stopped at the old man's store again," as the salesman tells the story. "I had forgotten all about that *no-idea, no-report* rule. But then I remembered it, and I knew that it was no use for me to go in unless I had an idea for the old man. I sat there for at least a half-hour before I could think of one that seemed worth trying. Then I went in. So help me, he didn't change a word, or a tone, or a facial expression. 'What's new?' he asked—and to this day I don't know whether he remembered me or not.

"I gave him my idea. It wasn't anything to get excited about. But it was new to him, and he seemed to like it. He gave me an order—quite a big order—and then he gave me an idea. He gave me one of the most valuable ideas I have ever had. He said, 'I don't know how good this idea of yours is—but that doesn't matter. What I want all of your salesmen to do is to keep bringing me ideas that can be tried out in this store. Most of them will not amount to much. Many of them won't be worth trying. But all of you salesmen get around and see what other stores are doing, and if enough of you bring me enough ideas that work for other stores, I'm going to get some good ones for this store. In fact, I've got a lot of good ones working now!'

"Each month after that I would pick out an idea for this old man before starting on my regular trip. Sometimes he liked the idea I brought, sometimes he didn't. But he always gave me an order. It was three or four months before I realized I had been handed a formula for success, and hadn't even looked at it.

"It was so simple. Other retailers didn't have this *idea-exchange* rule in the order department. But all retailers wanted practical merchandising ideas—or accounting ideas, or promotion ideas—they wanted *ideas,* period. So why not prepare a list of ideas before starting on each trip—not to offer them all to each customer, but to pick one to offer to each, fitted to his operation as nearly as I could do the fitting? The plan worked better than I expected—as I could have predicted if I had been more experienced. The ideas weren't so hot. But in trying to fit them to each customer's business, I had to think more about *his* business than I would have done otherwise . . . and any salesman who thinks about the customer's business, and shows that he is thinking of ways to help that business—entirely aside from sale of his own products—well, that salesman is half-way home!"

Lionel B. Moses reports the young salesman was convinced that the "no-idea, no-order" rule, developed and used with all his customers, was responsible for his appointment as district manager at least five years earlier than he would have reached this point without that help.

The bases, then, of creative sales presentations are (1) ideas to help the buyer, (2) presented in a novel way, and (3) presented persuasively. Here are some suggestions you may wish to adapt in developing and delivering your sales presentations.

Seven preliminaries

1. Select the account you're most eager to sell. It's probably the one that has the greatest potential for you. Then select the prospect with the second greatest potential, and so on, until you've covered your territory and sold all of them. Also develop the habit of giving an idea to each of your established accounts on every call.

2. Make a survey of each prospect's needs—how you can supply them. Sometimes you may have to go no further than this step. For example, John M. Wilson tells how one of his National Cash Register salesman surveyed bank tellers making out deposit slips for customers. He called on the president and said, "I notice that your tellers, Mr. Mills, prepare deposit slips for your customers. I was wondering on whom the burden of proof would fall if a depositor later claimed that he had deposited a greater amount than the total shown on his deposit ticket?" The president asked him to call back next day and gave him an order for an NCR savings system.

3. Gather information about the prospect's buying poli-

cies and procedures. Is the company buying from a competitor or competitors of yours? In what amounts? On what terms? How often? Can you submit a plan to save the company money? Can you help the company space its orders better? Suggest better control?

4. Compare and contrast your product with your competitor's. What advantages does your product have? (Any disadvantages? If so, what are the compensations?) If your product costs more, it probably is a superior product. Thus you sell the superiorities.

Thomas & Betts's, Karl G. Kemf, vice-president of marketing, describes the way his salesmen compete with price cutting. He calls it the "pink-screw" approach. This means that T&B's products must have that added something that makes them more distinctive, of better quality, and more versatile than competitive products. Thus, to compete with an iron electrical fitting with five screws, selling at 9 cents, T&B designs a steel fitting with only one screw. It sells for 10 cents. The T&B salesman emphasizes to a contractor that he can install the T&B fitting in one minute. The competitive fitting may require two minutes to install. With labor and overhead calculated at 10 cents a minute, the T&B fitting costs a contractor only 20 cents. The competitive fitting—selling for less—actually will cost 29 or more cents.

5. Compare and contrast the services you and your company provide with your competitor's services. (Ordinarily you do this without mentioning your competitor by name. For the professional salesman never degrades his competitors!) Perhaps you're selling a product exactly like your competitor's. It may be sugar, tetraethyl lead, or coal. You must then provide inducements to buy from you through superior advertising support, quicker delivery, and other services or advantages.

6. Find out who makes the buying decisions. One individual? Several? Separately or in committee? (In supermarket buying, for example, each buyer of a major line ordinarily is a member of a purchasing committee. The salesman must persuade the buyer and also indirectly help the buyer persuade the committee to take on the order.) In multilevel selling, where a number of individuals are involved—each making a decision alone—determine the proper sequence of your calls. Learn as much about these people and their decision-making habits as you can before approaching them.

7. Call on those who *help* make the buying decisions and in the order advantageous to you. (For example, a salesman sold a buyer a trial order of six engine preheaters for a New England trucking fleet. But the maintenance manager didn't have them installed. He objected to the time needed to attach them. Result: The salesman never sold units for all 104 trucks in the fleet. He neglected to educate the maintenance manager on how the preheaters actually save labor, assure quick starting in cold weather, reduce motor wear, add efficiency to the maintenance department; thereby, increase the prestige of the maintenance manager.)

These seven steps are easier to specify than to carry through. They involve a lot of planning, time, and resourcefulness. But the end results justify the effort.

The idea's the thing

Any idea you present the buyer that helps him sell more or make more profit, gain prestige, solve a problem, or make innovations that will help him be more competitive —is a creative idea and excellent psychology.

Here are 10 ideas taken from many that salesmen have used successfully in their selling.

1. A Canadian salesman taught a coal dealer's secretary to develop new retail accounts by telephone. He spent three hours rehearsing her with the aid of a voice recorder; showed her how to revivify lost accounts, sell additional services, such as furnace cleanings, installation of thermostat, coal-burning baskets for fireplaces, etc. Result: The salesman added an important dealer to his accounts.

2. Another salesman had a new line of colored soaps to sell through a supermarket chain. His plan involved a store-wide "Color Riot" with a proposed layout of props, window displays, tie-ins, and the local high school band.

3. A lumber salesman sold his dealers a lot of siding, trimming, and accessories for converting attics into service rooms. The salesman prepared advertising copy and a series of sales letters addressed to wives. One letter promoted the reconditioned attic as a sewing room; another, as a play room for children; still another as a den for the husband.

4. A sales representative for a trucking firm persuaded a glass manufacturer to switch from rail to truck. His approach was a study showing how his firm's specially padded and soft-spring trucks reduced breakage, lowered insurance rates.

5. A paper salesman analyzed his customers' (printers) production—showed how his papers took clearer images, dried faster, etc. His sales presentation was a series of double-page spreads. On the left page was the original; on the facing page, the same copy printed on his papers.

6. A New York banker's representative sold mortgages to members of a grange on the basis of soil analysis. These included recommendations for crop changes, soil conservation, and the like.

7. A Kleenex salesman sold a trainload of his product to a drug chain on the basis of a point-of-purchase sale. He arranged for the sale to be held on the same day in all

the chain's stores in his district. The point-of-purchase display took the form of a house. He and his fellow salesmen set up the same display in all the district stores. The "House of Kleenex" display was featured in the local papers. He also arranged to have a company salesman conduct each point-of-purchase sale.

8. An encyclopedia salesman increased his sales 300 per cent by speaking before parent-teacher associations and women's clubs. His topic was "Wonderful World of Teaching Machines." His examples and demonstrations were based on his encyclopedia. He showed how children received higher grades as a result of using encyclopedias.

9. A customer's man in a securities firm built a list of 400 active accounts. He helped organize investment clubs all over his county. Naturally, members bought their stocks and bonds from him.

10. A salesman of carpentry tools became extraordinarily successful in selling his complete line to independent hardware stores. To each owner he presented a floor plan designed to increase impulse buying. It's a rearrangement of his store on self-service principles. He showed how the new setup increased traffic, reduced labor, sold more carpentry tools!

In all these instances the salesmen were selling ideas to help their buyers or customers solve problems. The orders were the results. Sometimes you can use the same idea with all your customers; sometimes you can use one idea with several customers—usually noncompetitors; often you must provide a tailor-made plan or idea for each customer. For idea-producing hints, study the 19 suggestions in Chapter 16.

Marry logic with emotion in an avalanche

Memorize the benefits and advantages of your product. At the psychological moment you can then roll them off your tongue without tripping—the avalanche effect. For example, let's assume you're an Anchor Hocking Glass Corp. salesman. You're selling a merchandise manager, Anchorglass tumblers as the perfect premium. You may have to sell the buyer on adopting premiums before you specify glassware and your tumblers. And so. . . . "Mr. Arnold, as you know, premiums can help you in at least 13 ways." Here are the ways premiums can help to win customers:

1. They win sales in new markets and territories.
2. They offset price competition.
3. They introduce new products or packages.
4. They increase the unit sale.
5. They stimulate salesmen's enthusiasm.
6. They arouse dealer and distributor interest.
7. They secure better displays.
8. They spark special events.
9. They create consumer traffic.
10. They speed up sale of slow items.
11. They increase repeat sales.
12. They obtain new prospects.
13. They open new accounts.

If these reasons are stated with conviction, Mr. Arnold is impressed with your detailed analysis of what premiums may do for him.

You're now ready to imprint on his mind the fact that glassware is the best of all premiums for him at this time. "Let me take another minute, Mr. Arnold, to point out why glassware is the perfect premium for you at this time." You may then list for him these reasons:

1. Nothing else has the *universal appeal* of glassware.
2. It combines glamour with utility.
3. It induces pride of ownership.
4. It has inexhaustible appeal.

5. Glassware premiums stay in use as constant reminders of your product.

6. Glassware is one of the most *versatile* incentive choices.

7. Glassware premiums can be high, medium, or low-priced, personalized or plain, used in sets or as singles.

8. Glassware is perfectly adaptable to free point-of-sale gifts, self-liquidators, coupon redemptions, continuity promotions, accumulated register tape deals, dealer premium offers, salesmen's incentives, and many more.

9. Best of all, glassware premiums are always *low cost,* no matter how much you decide to spend.

10. Compare and you'll agree. No other merchandise can look so impressive or offer so much utility and eye appeal at such a low per-unit cost.

11. Glassware offers you the greatest value for your promotional value.

Once you have established in Mr. Arnold's mind the fact that premiums will help him sell his merchandise and that glassware is the ideal premium to meet his needs, you are ready to sell him your tumblers.

"May I suggest, Mr. Arnold, that of all Anchor Hocking Table Division's more than 2,000 items of household and related glassware—Anchorglass premium tumblers are fitted exactly to your needs. Think, if you will, how widely popular premium tumblers are. (Did you know the average family breaks more than 43 glasses a year?)" Your presentation may continue with these facts:

1. Anchorglass tumblers come in dozens of sizes and shapes.

2. As you see here, we have heavyweight or lightweight.

3. The glasses are frosted, clear, and in colors.

4. Glassware may be had personalized, plain, or in dozens of stock decorations.

5. Tumblers are machined or hand cut.

6. They may be used singly or in handy sets of four, six, or more.

7. All are adaptable to custom design or message.

8. All are available in small to very large quantities.

9. There is a wide price range.

(The sales points presented in this example are taken from an excellent advertisement of Anchor Hocking Glass Corp. in *Business Week*.)

Notice the logic in this presentation. You worked from the general to the specific. You began by establishing as your major premise the fact that premiums help Mr. Arnold sell his merchandise. You used as your minor premise the fact that glassware is the best kind of premium for him now. Third, you concluded that your tumblers are the natural, logical application of your two premises. Moreover, you did a lot more than just state the premises. You gave him 13 pieces of evidence to back up your first premise, 11 for your second, 9, for your conclusion.

You also aroused in him favorable feelings toward you and your ideas. Your logic made sense; your manner, speech, and visual aids were acceptable to him. The psychologist would say, "You created in him an *affective reaction*."

Creative sales presentations are persuasive in this sense: You base them on both logic and emotional appeal. And you deliver them without "uh's" or "er's" or other blocks. Mere ideas may fall on deaf ears unless presented contagiously—with sincerity, enthusiasm, conviction. (Remember: "A man convinced against his will is of the same opinion still.")

On the other hand, emotional appeal without logic usually repels the intelligent buyer, who justly prides himself on common sense.

Sell him six ways at once

Common complaint against salesmen is they talk without saying much and they don't listen. Actually, the criticism doesn't go far enough. For many salesmen neglect to plan their sales presentations to appeal to the buyer's *six* senses (or as many as the products or services permit). When you send out the same sales message to all six senses simultaneously, you may multiply your impact on the buyer's mind —by more than 600 per cent!

Therefore, when the professional salesman develops his sales presentations he asks himself, "In what specific ways will I stimulate all the buyer's senses to receive my sales message?"

1. *Auditory Sense.* "Are my voice, diction, tempo, word-flow persuasive to his ears?" (Record your sales presentations, play them back, practice them, perfect them.)

2. *Visual Sense.* "Is my appearance neat and pleasant to his eyes? Are my samples, visual aids, sales kit persuasive *images?*" (Practice handling your samples and visual aids before a mirror. Watch your movements as the buyer observes them. Perfect them and your gestures, facial expressions, and postures. Learn to handle your products and visuals without breaking eye contact with the buyer. Teach your fingers to find materials in your kit without looking for them. The mirror lets you play the roles of salesman and the buyer at the same time.)

3. *Tactile Sense.* "If my product or its package can be handled, do I present it to the buyer to let him *feel* it while I'm talking about it?" (When you feel it, do so with deference—"loverly." Your evident respect for it builds respect in the mind of the buyer!)

4. *Olfactory Sense.* "Does my product have a pleasant odor? If so, do I invite him to *smell* it?" (Many products these days are scented to appeal to the buyer's nose.)

5. *Gustatory Sense.* "Is my product demonstrable by *taste?* If so, do I suggest he follow my lead to taste it as I talk about it?"

6. *Kinesthetic Sense.* "Do I place my product (or visual aids) before him to greatest advantage—so that his sense of *position* and *equilibrium* are stimulated favorably? Also, am I aware that my sitting and standing postures (and gestures) have subtle, unconscious effects upon his kinesthetic sense?"

The professional salesman remembers that the (buyer's) mind is a stream—a myriad of ripples of ideas, sensations, both at conscious and unconscious levels. It's full of rapids and shoals and it never stands still. Constantly fed by the messages the salesman sends over the six senses, it's the greatest of divine currents.

Show and tell

If a picture—or other visual aid—is worth 10,000 words, then the professional salesman uses it. In planning his presentation, he decides whether to favor the sleek "boiler plate" provided by his company, his own homemade visuals, or a combination of both.

A survey we conducted among 100 buyers revealed that 92 said personalized visuals impressed them most. They referred to simple visuals salesmen made especially for them. One was merely a collection of seven consumer advertisements—with names of magazines in which they appeared—bound in a Manila folder with the buyer's name on it. The salesman leafed through it as he stood over the buyer's shoulder. Here was evidence of the company's current campaign to support distribution through the buyer's stores.

Another—voted best—deserves a thumbnail description. Made by a salesman of no artistic talent, it was a bright red folder—8½ by 11 inches. He bought it at his neighborhood "mama-and-papa" store. The inside had pockets—on either side—to hold pages. The salesman typed the pages with the highlights of his presentation. He wrote on the front cover with a flow brush (green):

Sales Plan

prepared for

Mr. JIM ARNOLD

Buyer of XYZ Co.

by

JOHN SMITH, *Sales Representative*

ABC Co.   (Date)

At the bottom John put the "logo" or seal of the XYZ Co.—cut from a brochure.

Inside the folder John had six typewritten pages—each a different tint—and an order blank with carbon ready for signing. He put all copy in capitals, generously indented and spaced. Here and there he underlined or framed an outstanding point with colored crayon. Two or three of the pages had illustrations, cutouts from magazines.

Each page contained the main points John made in his spoken presentation.

Page 1. The idea

Page 2. Advantages to Arnold in using the idea

Page 3. The plan—six steps to take in making the idea work

Page 4. The order needed to support the plan, also suggested schedule of shipments

Page 5. Specific ways John and his company planned to help the buyer at every stage—follow-up work

Page 6. The arithmetic—costs, savings, markups, profits to Arnold and his company.

On opening, John put the folder in Arnold's hands. He said, "To save you time, Mr. Arnold, here is a plan especially designed for you and XYZ Co. (As he went on, he handed Arnold the page talked about.)

Arnold saw *his* name as John pronounced it. He also saw *his* title, *his* company's name and "logo"—strongest appeal to arrest his attention and build his interest—*ego appeal*.

Before handing Arnold the next page, John said, "Do I make myself clear, Mr. Arnold?" (The break in the presentation built anticipation.) If Arnold said "Yes," John had built assent and agreement. If Arnold asked a question, raised an objection, or said "No"—John took advantage of it with *supplementary selling*.

When John ended his presentation, he gave Arnold the order blank, filled out, and handed him a pen to sign it. Then John put the six numbered pages in proper order in the right-hand pocket, Arnold's copy of the order in the left.

Notice that throughout the presentation, John had Arnold participating. He appealed to Arnold's logic and feelings through eyes, ears, sense of touch and kinesthetics. Moreover, John's showmanship aroused Arnold's admiration, built up his *attention, interest, desire, confidence*. He helped him to a *decision*, moved him to *action*, gave him a sense of *satisfaction*.

The professional salesman learns to use all sorts of visuals —flip charts, slides, films, the blackboard, demonstrations— in *conference selling* and to the *single buyer*. Often these aids are costly. Sometimes they're so stereotyped they leave the buyer cold. Usually the salesman can supplant them more impressively with simple personalized visuals, like the one just described.

Benefits from visuals

Among the less apparent benefits of the visual presentation are these:

1. Only rarely does the salesman have the pleasure of making uninterrupted presentations. Ringing telephones, office boys and secretaries, and a flock of other interruptions break into the interview. The visual helps the salesman win back the buyer's attention—preserves his memory of what went on before the break.

2. Even if the buyer doesn't sign the order, the visual left with him may continue to sell him after the salesman leaves. On the next call-back, the salesman may get the order. Moreover, the buyer will have increased respect for the salesman's method of doing business.

3. Some psychologists believe that many a buyer is a frustrated salesman. To have a personalized visual presentation help him—if necessary—persuade his committee, gives the salesman an enormous advantage.

4. Beyond all other benefits and advantages, the personalized visual presentation makes the salesman prepare and streamline his sales presentation. *Sales Management* recently surveyed buyer recommendations to salesmen. Said the largest number of buyers: "Salesmen should cut the time they take in making presentations by at least 50 per cent."

5. The planned presentation challenges the salesman to think through the exact size of the order he asks for. He has to prepare definite figures to include in the visual.

6. The personalized visual presentation forces the salesman to aim psychologically. It nudges him to think in

terms of strategy and tactics. When he prepares his presentation thoroughly, he organizes it around seven aspects of the buyer's mental stream:

a. Getting the buyer's *attention*
b. Building the buyer's *interest*
c. Arousing the buyer's *desire* to buy
d. Supporting and adding to the buyer's *confidence*
e. Helping the buyer to *decision* and *action*
f. Providing the buyer with *satisfaction*
g. Raising the buyer's *respect* for the salesman and his company.

In these seven ways, the professional salesman helps the buyer climb out of the valley of stones into the upland pastures of rich grazing.

Arnold Toynbee, the distinguished historian, has a message for creative salesmen when he says, "Apathy can only be overcome by enthusiasm, and enthusiasm can only be aroused by two things: first, an idea which takes the imagination by storm; and second, a definite intelligible plan for carrying that idea into practice!"

11

Two Dozen Courtesy Hints to Test and Develop Empathy

> The man who can put himself in the place of other men, who can understand the workings of their minds, need never worry about what the future has in store for him.
>
> OWEN D. YOUNG

Professional salesmen—like advertising specialists and other marketing experts—are excited these days about the concept of empathy. As you know, *empathy* is identifying yourself with the other fellow, his frame of mind, his emotions, his likes and dislikes, his quandaries. "Empathy" comes from the Greek and—interestingly enough—means "feeling pain with." It's a first cousin to "sympathy."

Whenever you talk with a customer, sensitive to his conditions, you're empathic. Whenever you devise an advertisement that makes the reader feel himself into it, you're empathic. Whenever you keep in mind your reader's reactions as you write him a letter, you're empathic. When you do such things—let's agree—you give yourself a big advantage. For then you can predict your customer's reactions, can serve him best.

Marks of the empathic salesman

Point to the empathic salesman and you see a man of keen sensibilities. His human relations excel; his common sense is enormous.

With or without formal education, to him the proper study of mankind is man. People are his specialty—how to analyze, interpret, and predict their actions and reactions. "People don't act, they only react," he says. Thus, through his study of others—and self-analysis as well—he knows human·nature. He's a keen student of manners and mannerisms, speech, facial expressions, gestures, postures, deportment—in short, how people use and respond to the customs of their environment.

When he develops empathy beyond the ordinary, he has perhaps the choicest of all personality traits. Empathy is the basis of popularity. It keeps company with intuition, personal magnetism, innate gentlemanliness. Without empathy, you can't have discernment and compassion.

Psychologists say empathy is strongest among those who like people and want to be liked by them. And, of course, you know that a man can't like others—or want to be liked by them—unless he respects and likes himself.

How to develop empathy

Can empathy be developed? The answer is "Yes." Courtesy is at once a reflection and developer of empathy.

The salesman of high purpose, therefore, practices courtesy to, develop empathy. He's interested to review, for example, the 24 "do's and don'ts" most often named by buyers when asked to advise salesmen about manners and sales etiquette. You may want to use them as a check list. At one time, they serve two purposes: a measurement of your own genteel habits, and developers of empathy. Here they are:

1. *Keep appointments promptly.* The most precious commodity to busy men or women is time. They have so many profitable ways to invest it. When a salesman keeps a customer waiting, he gives a bad impression—of poor work habits, thoughtlessness, disregard for the buyer's schedule. Actually, the tardy salesman creates a buyer's resistance to his sales presentation—by being late. If he's unavoidably detained, he telephones the buyer ahead of the appointment to explain and apologize—and asks if he may come late or at another time. The high-level salesman arrives at least five minutes ahead of his appointment. If he must wait beyond the appointed time, he doesn't fret or create a disturbance. Rather, he makes use of the extra minutes in reading, doing his paper work, planning, reviewing his presentation, etc.

2. *Dress neatly.* The salesman's appearance bespeaks his company and the products or services he sells—as well as himself. He's sure to follow his company's policy in matters of dress and appearance. If he sells in a warm climate, he doesn't wear a T shirt on a sales call—when company policy demands a tie and jacket. He's fastidious—nice to be near. He wisely carries a deodorant, hair tonic, and razor in his kit—to freshen up throughout the day.

Most topnotch salesmen wear hats. It helps to give them assurance and status. It lends a bit of formality and deference to their calls. It is tipped, taken off, put on, held, hung up, brushed, cleaned, renewed—at the right times.

A sales manager recently invited one of his young salesmen to attend a sales executive club luncheon. The young salesman appeared in a loud jacket with his shirt collar turned down—to the embarrassment of his manager. Until the manager spoke to him about it, the salesman was blind to the incongruity. High-level salesmen observe how successful salesmen and sales executives dress—and guide themselves accordingly.

3. *Use quality language.* The words the salesman uses reveal what kind of person he is. Dr. Wilfred Funk, word expert, says, "In an average and normal day, if you are an articulate person, you will talk an estimated 30,000 words. And these words will reveal *you* to your listener—your mental processes, your character, your ability, your personality." How particularly true this is of salesmen, most of whom speak more than 30,000 words daily!

The professional salesman favors the level of language used by the educated people of his community. It is simple, not ostentatious; colloquial, not too slangy; grammatical, not crude; sparkling, not pedantic.

Obviously, he avoids cursing, swearing, and the use of filthy language. For he knows it reveals sewage of the mind. The professional salesman "minds his speech lest it mar his fortune." He checks up on the quality of the language he uses daily.

4. *Mind your posture.* Have you ever walked into a waiting room and noticed the sprawled out postures? Sometimes you have to pick your way gingerly to avoid tripping. The topnotch salesman doesn't have to be reminded of sprawling; nor of the impact of good posture on the buyer. He doesn't lean or sit on the buyer's desk—and certainly doesn't prop his feet on it or a chair. Neither does he sit unless he's invited to do so. Ordinarily he sits straight and quiet—to help sustain the buyer's attention. In walking,

his posture is straight—to reflect confidence and vigor, to help him carry the heavy burden of his day lightly.

5. *Make use of pleasant facial expressions*. They are the conveyors of visible messages. As the result of tension, an occasional salesman develops nervous twitches, a squint, or habitual frowning. These, of course, beget negative buyer reactions. Perhaps an occasional session before a mirror would help such a salesman—talking aloud as he watches himself.

In the sales interview, the salesman's facial expression responds sympathetically as he listens. It also enriches the meanings of the words he speaks. Whether he's saying "Good morning!" "I'm sorry to hear that," "You can be sure, Mr. Smith," his face reflects his attitude as well as the meaning of the words.

And he smiles readily and sincerely. As sales manager Harry Sheerin says, "A smile should be easy to negotiate; it is standard equipment, even with the grouchiest of us. It is almost never overused. It never wears out. Indeed, it seems to grow brighter and more lovely with use."

6. *Listen well*. Salesmen should learn to listen as energetically as they talk. Many salesmen most of the time are chiefly concerned with getting their own views across. They tend to find the customer's remarks tedious interruptions. (At least many customers believe this.)

Good listening implies normal hearing—or an adequate substitute. Good listening also means trying to see the problem the way the speaker sees it. The alert salesman enters actively and imaginatively into the buyer's situation. Good listening means not only trying to see the other fellow's point of view, but momentarily sharing it with him.

Buyers stress two listening faults of salesmen. In the one the salesman replies before the buyer has finished speaking. In the second, the salesman delays too long in answering. And as he delays he stares at the buyer or elsewhere. Here the timing of the response is important etiquette and excellent psychology.

A closely related problem is asking others to repeat unnecessarily. This is often caused by deafness of which the salesman may be unaware. If the salesman discovers himself repeating, "What did you say?" he has a signal to get his hearing tested.

7. *Avoid nervous mannerisms.* Psychologists have counted approximately 150 nervous mannerisms or *autistic gestures.* These recurrent, involuntary movements ordinarily take place in speaking—the speaker seemingly unaware that he has them. Examples are twitching, tugging at the collar, tapping, joint cracking, blinking. They distract the attention of the buyer, often make him nervous. Any salesman having one or more of them should seek expert help.

Closely related to autistic gestures are unpleasant personal habits such as nose picking, shifting false teeth, head scratching, and the like. They are done unconsciously. Until brought to a conscious level—by a friend or self-analysis—they're not likely to be broken.

8. *Don't be loud.* Because of the great noise in which most of us live, voices are getting loud and strident. Buyers say salesmen often talk in an office as if they were shouting across the street. In the first place, the buyer ordinarily likes as much quiet as he can get. In the second place, he often wants to hold his interviews in some confidence. The loud speaker therefore irritates him. Quite often customers mention bragging in the same breath with loudness. Typically, loudness accompanies braggadocio. Both are affronts to the customer's ego and, of course, should be avoided or corrected. Sales executive S. A. Madsen once said, "Some people will believe almost anything if you whisper."

9. *Address others in a friendly but not overly familiar way.* An elderly woman once chided the young Winston Churchill with the words, "Familiarity breeds contempt!" To which he replied, "Ah, yes, Madam, but I don't know how you can breed anything without a certain degree of familiarity." Perhaps for our purposes the word "degree" is the most meaningful in Sir Winston's classic remark.

In the past, salesmen were accused of being too breezy and familiar. Today, professional salesmen play the role of responsible businessmen. They address their customers by "Mr.," "Mrs.," or "Miss"—unless invited to use their first names. The formal address in no way detracts from friendliness, yet preserves the advantage of deference.

Many salesmen don't use the customer's name often enough throughout a sales presentation. Occasionally, however, you can hear one that overuses the customer's name in direct address. In certain sections of the United States salesmen use "Sir," "Yes, sir," and "No, sir," throughout the presentation. The best advice is to use direct address often enough to make a pleasing but not oily impression on the listener.

10. *Show deference.* Buyers recommend to salesmen that they be deferential. Perhaps a better way to express it is —be thoughtful of the ego and comfort of others. And there are hundreds of gracious ways to express deference —letting him or her go first, asking permission to raise or lower a window before doing so, offering him a preference, holding a door, expressing kindness without condescension, and so on.

To be deferential to one in high position is, of course, natural—and an easy thing to do. To be deferential to the defenseless, the less secure, the subservient—this is a constant challenge to all gentlemen.

11. *"Don't doubt my word!"* You don't expect, of course,

to hear "That's a lie!" "You're crazy!" or "That's not so!"
—although buyers report they hear such expressions oftener
than we imagine. The professional salesman rarely uses
the "meat-ax" approach. You never hear him say, "You're
wrong," "I don't believe that," "You don't mean what you
say." Rather, he parries statements he can't accept with this:
"What you say may well be right, Mr. Jones, but may I
suggest . . ." This velvet-glove approach smooths ruffled
feathers. It prevents explosions. It helps the salesman reach
his goal. With this approach one can agree with his ad-
versary and yet make his point—often in a winning way,
too!

12. *Be polite to secretaries and receptionists.* They are
often the boss's boss. They can help a salesman. They de-
serve courteous treatment. Studies indicate that the vast
majority of secretaries queried say they prefer a salesman
who (*a*) takes off his hat before entering the office; (*b*) speaks
without a cigarette or cigar in his mouth; (*c*) greets you
pleasantly but not in a flippant way; (*d*) asks for help rather
than demands service; (*e*) doesn't argue when a request
isn't granted; (*f*) doesn't ask to use the company phone for
his personal business; (*g*) expresses thanks.

The salesman who observes these secretarial preferences
—and adds to them the other courtesy hints—should go far
to win as a friend the buyer's secretary.

13. *Don't smoke unless invited to do so.* Of course, the
alert salesman doesn't smoke as he enters the customer's
presence. This is taking liberties. It reflects overfamiliarity.
Smoking may irritate the customer or prospect. He may
not approve of it. A good rule for the professional salesman to observe is this: Don't smoke unless you're invited
to do so. Do so then only if you enjoy it and if it will not
detract from your sales presentation. If you don't care to
smoke, say something like, "Thank you, Mr. Smith, may I

be excused? I'm trying to help a cough go away..."

If, on the other hand—so the tried rule goes—you enjoy smoking, and smoking with the buyer will help create a bond—by all means smoke. Offer him a light. And when you're through, ask him if you may empty the ash tray into the wastebasket.

14. *Don't drink on the job; sparingly off the job, if at all.* One of our leading sales executives today tells the lesson he learned as a rookie salesman. He called on an elderly prospect in Minneapolis one cold afternoon—right after lunch. The young fellow had had a cocktail. The sharp-nosed old man, after the greeting, said, "Young fellow, I never talk business with a man who's been drinking. If you want, come to see me another time. My girl will give you an appointment. Good day!"

"This wonderful experience came at the right time in my career!" says the sales executive. "Since then I've made it a rule never to make a sales call with liquor on my breath."

Social drinking among salesmen is, of course, widespread. Cocktails and highballs are often served at luncheons, dinners, parties. Many sales meetings are spaced with festive affairs. All these situations are tests of courteous behavior. To those who drink, the concept of the *personal equation* is an excellent challenge. Salesmen A discovers that he can drink one martini and retain all his desirable social inhibitions. But if he drinks two or more, he loses control of his tongue and deportment. He has met his personal equation with one martini. As a wise man, *he* never exceeds one.

Now Salesman B has a high tolerance for alcohol. He can drink scotch and soda far into the night—and remain in control of himself. His personal equation is different from Salesman A's.

The intelligent salesman—if he drinks at all—never drinks before making calls; and drinks socially within his personal equation.

Many salesmen who don't wish to drink alcoholic beverages—yet want to be sociable—have discovered the "Horse's Neck." As you know, it's a tall glass of ginger ale with a long piece of lemon rind clinging to the glass. It looks like a particularly rakish highball, yet is as innocent as a baby's stare. To the uninitiated, the order "Give me a 'Horse's Neck,' " sounds interesting too.

15. *Be careful of the stories you tell.* The empathic salesman knows that his stories measure his sense of propriety. He's careful to tell his stories discreetly. Someone has said, "Nothing more surely kills a nascent admiration; nothing causes more distaste or sense of affront than to have an improper story—no matter how funny—forced on you by one from whom you are not ready to hear it."

On the other hand, a slightly risqué story marks a heightened relationship between urbane people. It ordinarily indicates a closer bond of friendship. The good conversationalist, therefore, selects his stories judiciously—sharing certain ones with some, certain others with some others.

Some of our greatest salesmen tell wonderful stories. Like Abraham Lincoln's or Will Rogers's or Bennett Cerf's, the stories are delightful and free of bad taste.

16. *Be a good conversationalist.* Is there any skill more enjoyable or profitable? The professional salesman in the course of his work has many opportunities to profit from conversation. It's a source of contacts, information, and study of human nature. Conversation is one of the best adventures in empathy. What is salesmanship but conversation plus demonstration?

The professional salesman studies to improve his conversation. He also studies the essence of good conversation. He learns to draw others out rather than monopolize the talk. He learns too what it isn't: It isn't an argument or a debate or a harangue. There should be no quarrels —although genial disagreement is welcome.

It is a give-and-take affair. At its best, it takes place among six or eight—a small enough group for each one to have some contact with all the others. If he is the host, our salesman should act as a catalyst, blending the ideas of his guests—keeping them happy and free from boredom or tension.

Why is so much conversation dull and unrewarding? Why do so many salesmen fail to capitalize on their personality assets in social conversation?

Sydney J. Harris, distinguished newspaper columnist, answers these questions. He says fear is to blame—points up four manifestations of fear especially:

a. Fear of being wrong or being thought ignorant. Some personalities are so fragile that they cannot stand the possibility of being contradicted or controverted, so they say as little as possible, and confine themselves to insipid generalities.

b. Fear of being original or different. The herd impulse is frightfully strong in this land of alleged individualists, and the need to conform to standard patterns of belief prevents many persons from voicing any amusing or significant deviations they might secretly feel.

c. Fear of being dull. Paradoxically enough, the most important factor in *creating* dullness is the fear of saying daring or witty things that might fall flat—so dullness becomes a defense against itself.

d. Fear of exploration or profundity. Many persons live in so precarious an emotional balance that they feel they cannot afford to discuss anything that might question their fundamental attitudes. Any conversation that goes deeper than superficiality is shunned by them as possibly leading to a dangerous self-examination or self-accusation.

Of course, there are persons who are congenitally dull, who simply are not interesting because they are not interested, who make no demands upon themselves because they make none on the world. But these, I am convinced, are in a small minority.

The first goal, then, is to get rid of the fears Sydney J. Harris describes. Perhaps the best way to do this is by association, that is, keep admirable company—with men and women who practice the art of conversation. Their sweet contagion will take hold.

17. *Be at home in polite society.* Buyers are often entertained by salesmen—sometimes on a grand scale. They report they are particularly impressed by young salesmen who are deft in making introductions. Such salesmen follow the simple formula of, in mixed company, asking the lady's permission to introduce the man. Thus, "Mrs. White, may I introduce Mr. Jones?" At stag affairs, they ask the older—more honored—individual's permission to introduce the younger. Thus, "President Green, may I introduce my friend, Jack Black?"

When the salesman takes the initiative—in an unheralded way—to introduce others in a group, he does several things. He helps to integrate the group, thereby creating a climate of friendliness. He makes sure the shy and hesitant feel wanted. He reveals himself as an outgoing person —thoughtful of the welfare of others.

18. *Watch your table manners.* A famous editor says he can tell more about a man just by observing him dine in company than any other way. If he is the host, how he looks after their needs and wishes. How he passes food

before partaking himself. How he waits—if he is a guest —to begin a course until his host starts. How he avoids reaching. How he manages his knife and fork, his arms and elbows. How neat he keeps the place before him. How he treats the waiter—never bawling him out or calling to him from a distance. How he tips him without vulgar display. How he alternates eating with conversation—of course, not talking with food in the mouth. How he avoids unpleasant or squeamish subjects at the table. Such hints as our editor friend gives are like carrying coals to New- castle—to the gentleman-salesman.

19. *Remember telephone courtesy too.* Buyers—because they use the telephone a lot—are sensitive to good telephone manners. The New York Telephone Company asks 14 questions to help guide us in telephone courtesy. They are excellent reminders:

a. When telephone rings, do you answer immediately?

b. Do you give the company name and your name when you answer?

c. Do you speak directly into the transmitter in a normal tone of voice?

d. Do you have a pencil, an order pad, and price lists right at hand, so that you won't have to leave the phone?

e. When it is necessary for you to leave the line, do you explain to the customer that you have to step away and then set the receiver down gently?

f. When you return to the line, do you say, "Thank you for waiting," or some other courteous introductory remark?

g. Do you address the customer by name as often as possible during the conversation?

h. When you indicate to the customer that you will call back, do you keep the promise as soon as possible?

i. When you receive a call for someone who is out, do you offer to take a message?

  j. Do you listen attentively without interrupting?
  k. When placing a call, do you have in mind exactly what
     you want to say?
  l. When the customer answers the phone, do you identify
     yourself immediately?
  m. As the call is being terminated, do you thank the cus-
     tomer and reassure him that his order will be filled
     promptly?
  n. Do you wait for the customer to hang up first, and then
     replace your receiver gently?

   20. *Watch your temper.* Psychologists tell us that temper
is a sign of defeat. When we have a temper tantrum, we
admit we can't solve the problem. We shut off common
sense and turn on the flow of adrenaline. Buyers, because
they're usually in the driver's seat, can be frustrating. Some
of them actually egg a salesman on. If they can rattle him
they have the upper hand. And so, temper outbursts—aside
from being childish and discourteous—put the salesman
at a disadvantage. By planning the sales presentation carefully—by being confident—by constantly developing a
sense of humor, the professional salesman learns to keep his
temper under control.
   21. *Acknowledge communications promptly.* Letters,
memos, telephone calls should be answered as quickly as
possible. It's good business to do so, and excellent manners.
Delays cause tensions, doubts, and often involve unhappi-
ness or frustration for many people. The empathic salesman is sensitive to the impact of procrastination on others.
He is unselfish and cooperative enough to keep up to date
in his communications.
   22. *Keep that promise.* A gentleman is one who keeps his
word. This is what buyers have in mind when they say:
"Keep your promise." This basic courtesy is the backbone
of business, the essence of character, the mark of emotional

maturity. To the professional salesman, a promise is as inviolate as a legal contract.

23. *Say "thank you."* Dr. Morse DellPlain, president of The Welsbach Corporation, recently wrote a beautiful editorial for his company's magazine—*The Welsbach Family.* It dealt with prayer. Morse DellPlain said, "The greatest of all prayers is *thank you.*" To be really grateful one must feel the urge to express gratitude and then express it. The empathic salesman feels gratitude for the opportunity to sell, for orders, for all the other blessings and kindnesses that come his way.

24. *Say "good-by."* An occasional complaint of buyers is that the salesman leaves abruptly, doesn't terminate the interview in a definitely gracious way. All of us have met the inconsistent fellow who sometimes greets you and sometimes says good-by and sometimes doesn't. Even when preoccupied, let your deeply ingrained habits to express greetings and farewells prevail.

There are, of course, many other courtesy hints that we can glean through observation. We can make them our own through practice. And the professional, the empathic salesman keeps his human relations tuned to courtesy— at all times.

He is adaptable in social situations. He uses as his headlamps *tact* and *humor*—tact, the sense of proportion; humor, the sense of disproportion. By steering his way with their constant light, he never deviates into sarcasm or grossness.

He is high-minded, agreeing with Cardinal Newman's observation that a gentleman is one who never knowingly inflicts pain. He is quick and wise to see that the spirit of courtesy and empathy reside in the golden rule. "Do unto others as you would have them do unto you," is perhaps the best of all guides to courtesy. Whenever he is in doubt about what to do, the professional salesman refers to the golden rule. It makes for the best courtesy—the surest empathy. It is the finest motto for the gracious heart.

Lights in the church

In Switzerland there's a little church—built in lawless days centuries ago. It has no windows, neither has it any lights. The villagers who attend service there follow an ancient, pleasant custom. Each one carries into the church a candle, taper, or lantern. And as he stands—for there are no pews, only a few chairs at the sides for the infirm—his light shines throughout the service.

Just as the Swiss villagers carry their lights into the little old church, so professional salesmen carry the candle of courtesy, the taper of tolerance, the lantern of lasting kindness wherever they live and work.

12

The Importance of the Little Things in High-level Selling

> I do not believe that a person who ignores the small things of life, the small truths, the small decencies, the small pleasantnesses, the small graciousness, can undertake anything in a big way.
>
> NEHRU

Big trees from little acorns

To be a professional salesman you must be attentive to the little things. You must know that mind and heart respond to the engaging word, the polite manner, the offhand favor, the kindly deed, the gracious heart. You must be alert to the impact of stimuli—of your appearance, deportment, and sales presentation—on the mind of the buyer. You must take infinite pains not to neglect the little things. For you know and believe that little things have big consequences.

The sales manager wields the broom

A sales manager and one of his salesmen made a joint call on a supermarket. They wanted to get more shelf space

151

for their product. The supermarket manager said he was too busy to see them.

The sales manager and his salesman noticed a stock boy stacking canned peas on the shelf. The loudspeaker called the stock boy to the front of the store. While he was gone, the salesman filled the shelf with canned peas. The sales manager—seeing a broom in the corner—swept the aisle. When the stock boy returned, he couldn't believe his eyes. A salesman helping him! A sales manager—a big shot—sweeping the aisle? Of course, the word spread.

Even the supermarket manager came over to have a look. He too was impressed. He couldn't resist the suggestion to give more shelf space to the salesman's product. A little thing, or should we say a thing?

John H. Patterson and the two-by-fours

John H. Patterson—so-called father of sales training in the United States—used to make surprise visits throughout his National Cash Register Co. One day he looked in on the packing department. He saw a man sawing two two-by-fours—one on top of the other—at a band saw. (Always before, he had seen one two-by-four sawed at a time.)

"How did you learn to do this?" the old gentleman asked. "Oh," replied the fellow, "Jack Barringer, our foreman, taught us to do that. He said we could saw twice as much at no extra effort."

John H. Patterson promoted Jack Barringer then and there. That was the first step in a series of promotions for him. It ended in Barringer's becoming vice-president of sales for NCR. A little thing?

Dale Carnegie and the drug buyer

A salesman tried to see a buyer of a drugstore chain. The buyer didn't want to see him. He was angry at the company the salesman represented. Our salesman friend learned that the buyer was taking the Dale Carnegie course in public speaking. The salesman wrote the buyer a personal note. He offered to share some speech-training materials from his training program. His approach was this: Perhaps the buyer would like to have copies of the materials for his staff. Of course, the buyer was interested. The salesman got in and got the order. He did more, he established good relations between the buyer and the salesman's company. Notice how all this resulted from a little thing.

The coal salesman and the clipping

Then there's the instance of the coal salesman. He had no better product, price, or service to offer a utility company. And the buyer was content with his one source of supply. How to break the impasse?

The salesman read in the local newspaper that the buyer's son became captain of his high school ball team. The salesman wrote the buyer a note of congratulations with the article enclosed. Next time he called on the buyer the welcome mat was out. And the salesman got a token order. In time, the order grew to half the utility's annual tonnage. Notice how a little thing started the ball rolling in the salesman's direction.

Courtesy with Kleenex

George E. Darden, sales manager in Texas for a large paper company, teaches his salesmen the value of little things. He trains them in the distinctive courtesies of selling. For example, when a Darden salesman leaves the buyer's desk—if they have been smoking—the salesman says, "May I?" He then empties the ash tray into the wastebasket; takes a piece of Kleenex from his pocket, and wipes out the tray. Such little courtesies help make his salesmen "the one man in twenty."

What buyers like and dislike about salesmen

The American Lumberman collected from dealers their likes and dislikes as regards salesmen. The results are a valuable check list of little things (but, oh, how important!) that hinder or promote sales. Dealers *dislike* a salesman who:

1. Overpromises and oversells.
2. Misrepresents and exaggerates.
3. Abuses telephone privileges.
4. Talks prices in front of my customers.
5. Sells my customers without my consent.
6. Carries tales.
7. Tries to "buy" my business.
8. Interrupts me when I am obviously busy.
9. Parks in my customers' parking lot.
10. Is careless of his language and with my time.

Dealers *like* a salesman who:

1. Respects my time.
2. Talks about "us" instead of his company.
3. Tells me how his product serves my needs.
4. Knows his products.
5. Helps us train our employees to sell his products.
6. Calls upon our trade only with our specific consent.
7. Lives up to his promises.
8. Does not inventory our needs without our consent.
9. Talks about our specific problems rather than general dealer problems.
10. Is courteous and careful of his appearance.
11. Calls on us at our convenience.
12. Spells and pronounces my name and the company name correctly.
13. Can step up— Speak up— Shut up!

Little things build morale

Sales managers know the value of the little things in building morale. Joe E. Blakemore, sales manager in Kansas City for a consumer-products company—has trained his salesmen to do a very gracious thing. Each time a new salesman comes into the division, he is made to feel wanted in very definite ways. For example, when he registers at the hotel he is handed a note of welcome from each of his fellow salesmen in the division—men he's not yet met. On the same day the new salesman's wife receives a bouquet of American Beauties from Joe Blakemore and the salesmen. These little things make a tremendous impact on the salesman and his family.

The manager who won by washing windows

A friend was a variety store manager in Georgia during World War II. The manager would get to work by 6:30 A.M. once a week—to wash the store windows. The president of the variety chain drove by one morning as the manager was doing the humble chore. Upon returning to New York from his vacation, the president summoned the store manager to the home office.

"I saw you washing the store windows one morning last month. Why were *you* doing it?" he asked.

"I was short-handed," he said. "You see, we try to maintain standards even if we have to work a little harder—all of us—down in Georgia."

Our friend was invited to stay in New York. Today he is merchandise manager of the whole chain of variety stores. What if he hadn't taken the trouble to do the humble task?

A salesman of business directories—selling on commission—makes good use of personalized post cards. They bear his facsimile signature cater-cornered at the top. After each call he sends a note of thanks for the time the customer or prospect gave him. The salesman believes that this little thing does more for his sales than any other single factor. "They tell me I'm the only one that goes to the trouble," he says.

The bank V-P and the majorettes

Foster R. Clement, Jr. is a vice-president of New York's Chase Manhattan Bank—the nation's second largest in deposits. Clement is a professional salesman; his territory is Illinois where he persuades the state's country banks to let Chase represent them in New York as "correspondent bank."

Clement recalls that a country banker once wrote asking for two drum majorettes to appear in a convention parade. It seems a local American Legion post band was due to appear in New York but couldn't afford to send the girls and their chaperones. "Some banks might have thrown the letter away," says Clement, "but we didn't, and we found the girls—one on Long Island and the other in New Jersey." He adds: "If you think any other bank will ever take that account away from us, you're crazy."

Chase Manhattan accents service; admits that the key factor in winning or losing business—even in this era of scientific management—is still the personality of the man in the field making calls. Chase holds regular briefings for all its salesmen—on monetary policy, new production methods, etc. But still it has to depend on the grass-roots touch and kindly services of its representatives. As Clement says: "A man has to be able to talk the language of these country bankers if he's going to get anywhere. He's got to remember faces, the president's wife's name, the names of his kids, and his secretary. It's the little things that count."

Thomas J. Watson's grace notes

One of America's greatest salesmen, the late Thomas J. Watson of IBM, used to encourage his executives to write notes of congratulations and condolence on personal stationery. He knew they meant more than dictated, typed letters.

"Grace notes," he called them! What a fitting description! For just as the grace notes add beauty and enrichment to the theme of a symphony, so do the little things add luster to salesmanship.

The salesman at close quarters

Observe outstanding salesmen at close quarters. Notice how distinctive—without being eccentric—they and their operation are. "Neatest man I ever saw! Always looks as if he stepped out of a bandbox! Never knew a man to have so many friends! Always has time for a smile and a friendly word! The secretaries are always on his side! Knows the interests and hobbies of all his customers! Phones his wife every night when he's on the road! Never forgets to send you a birthday card! Always knows someone or some way to help you out! He makes you feel good every time you talk with him! Always has a helpful suggestion!"

Such exclamations testify to the importance of the little things. But in the long run are they little? Certainly their consequences are often huge. Psychologists have discovered that in the great area of human relations, the so-called little things are often the most important things. Successful salesmen—most practical students of psychology—know this well indeed.

And so, to the salesman who sets his goals high—and works faithfully to achieve them—the little things take on vast importance. He cultivates their use and benefits by imposing 10 directives on himself.

Ten ways to cultivate the little things

Assignment

1. Recall in detail the little things—seemingly insignificant happenstances—in your own experience that have changed your life or the lives of others. Make a list of them to impress upon your own mind their import. This is an excellent way to deepen respect for the significance of the little things.

2. Build an inventory of all the little things you have done or can do for your customers. Constantly add to your list. Find out from other salesmen what gratuitous services and favors they extend. Suggest to your sales manager that "The Importance of the Little Things" might make an excellent discussion subject for a sales meeting. (A group of 20 salesmen recently listed 202 specific "little things" that they used advantageously in promoting their sales.) Through such an exchange of ideas, everyone on the team benefits.

3. Make use of one "little thing" on each of your calls on every customer. You build distinction that way—bind him to you with hoops of gratitude.

4. Keep a record of the little things you use with each customer. Don't trust to memory. He'll be impressed with the variety of grace notes in your symphony.

5. Don't use little things as substitutes for well-planned sales presentations, promotional or merchandising ideas. Use them as supplements. The professional salesman never sells on favors alone.

6. Aim each little thing at a customer's needs, desires, interests. You give and get more benefits that way.

7. Be generous-minded in extending the little things. Don't be a horse trader. Get joy out of going the extra mile, giving the baker's dozen. Don't put the generous deed on the basis of "I'll do this for you if you'll do that for me."

8. Study the effect of faithfully doing the little things on your own attitudes—personality—character. You grow in job joy by doing so.

9. Read biographies of great salesmen and others noted for their accomplishments. Notice the significant part that the little things play in their lives.

10. Deepen your respect for the basic law of life—the law of cause and effect—by observing the results of little things. You may not always be able to predetermine the effects of a little thing. But you know that every action brings on a chain of reactions: from good comes good.

Lamb chops and old maids

The great Charles Darwin, author of *Origin of Species* and other great books, a hundred years ago used an amusing example of cause and effect. He proved a relationship between the number of old maids living in England at that time and the price of lamb chops. How did he do it?

Here's how. The more old maids you have, the more cats you have. The more cats you have, the more cats you put out at night. The more cats you put out at night, the fewer mice and rats you have. The fewer mice and rats you have, the fewer beehives are robbed. The fewer beehives robbed, the more bees you have. The more bees you have, the more pollen is carried into the pastures. The more pollen carried into the pastures, the richer, the more plentiful the pasturage grows. The richer, the more plentiful the pasturage, the more food the lambs eat. The more food the lambs eat, the faster they grow—the more meat they put on their bones—

thus giving you an increased supply of meat. The more meat you have, the lower its price.

Therefore, the more old maids you have, the lower the price of lamb chops.

Good human relations have good motives

Just as the law of cause and effect prevailed with the old maids and the lamb chops—so does it have its way universally. The professional salesman studies its marvelous manifestation as he practices the gracious little things in his work. They help him to sell well.

They bring him much happiness too, particularly when conceived rightly. He doesn't go along with many people today who practice gracious actions for ulterior motives. Nor does he think of good human relations as tricks to make others do what he wants them to do—a kind of occult psychology to pull the strings and make the puppets dance accordingly.

Rather, his point of view has roots in his belief in the dignity of the individual. And from those roots he grows words and deeds to bring forth the best in others regardless of ulterior rewards to himself.

The grouchy newsboy and the decent chap

You may know the story Sydney Harris tells about a neighbor of his in a Chicago suburb. Three or four days in a row they lined up together to buy their newspapers as they waited for the train. Harris observed that his neighbor always said "Good morning," to the newsboy and thanked him for making change. The newsboy—long since of voting age—never acknowledged the greeting or the thank you. He was the cross, growling type.

Harris finally said to his neighbor, "Why do you continue

to treat that surly newsboy so politely? I notice he never responds civilly."

"Why shouldn't I?" replied the neighbor. "Shall I let his bad manners dictate the kind I should use?"

The neighbor's attitude, I believe, illustrates the point of view of the professional salesman. His contacts with others always present the challenge of treating people graciously—whether their adjustment permits them to deal decently with others or not.

PART 3

Personal Progress for Professional Salesmen

13

How to Burn the Midnight Oil Profitably

What instruction is more effectual than self-instruction?

THACKERAY

What to study

Ambitious salesmen ask themselves—and others—"What should I study to advance myself in my profession?" The answer to this intelligent question depends upon your background and aims. It depends also upon your specialized interest in selling. As you know, salesmanship is a much broader field now than formerly. Professionally minded salesmen think of themselves as marketing specialists. They increasingly call themselves "marketers," since the work they do supplements so many specialized marketing activities.

Their interests and duties therefore cover interrelated fields, such as direct selling, sales promotion, merchandising, advertising, consumer and motivational research, distribution, packaging, product management, sales manage-

165

ment, and the like. Moreover, most marketing divisions—
and the departments reporting to them—are headed by
former direct salesmen, salesmen who prepared themselves
for other marketing activities.

One of the first things to do is to study your company's
marketing organization. A good way to begin is to match
the usual definitions with your company's use of them in
practice. For example, some companies combine merchandising and sales promotion in one department. Others
separate them and assign specific functions to each.

Ruth Vogel, executive vice-president of A&P's National
Bakery Division, conceives of marketing in eight divisions.
These are (1) advertising; (2) consumer research; (3) market research; (4) merchandising; (5) motivational research;
(6) product or brand management; (7) sales promotion; and
(8) salesmanship. Let's use Ruth Vogel's recommended
divisions and define the first seven of them.

Definitions of marketing activities

1. *Advertising.* According to American Marketing Association, advertising is "any paid form of non-personal
presentation and promotion of ideas, goods or services by
an identified sponsor. It involves the use of such media as
the following: magazine and newspaper space, motion pictures, outdoor displays (posters, billboards, skywriting,
signs, etc.), direct mail, store signs, novelties (calendars,
blotters, etc.), radio and television, cards (car, bus, etc.),
catalogues, directories and references, programs and menus,
and circulars." Last year the United States spent a reported
11 billion dollars in advertising. "Over the next 10 years,
American advertising will grow by as many dollars as it
reached in all the years since Benjamin Franklin (180 years

of growth in 10). Even assuming no inflation the level will be raised to 22 billion." This remarkable prediction comes from Marion Harper, Jr.—president and chairman of McCann-Erickson, Inc.

2. *Consumer research*. This includes activities and studies to discover what consumers like or dislike about a product or service; what new products or new features (added to established products) they want. These activities are carried out through questionnaires, interviews, or canvassing of panels of consumers, etc.

3. *Market research*. Studies of distribution of sales territories, products, and product acceptance, market share trends, evaluation of product or service packaging, advertising effectiveness, productivity, profitability, competitive moves, etc., are included. In many companies market research includes consumer and motivational research. In others, these are farmed out to consulting organizations.

4. *Merchandising*. This covers activities aimed at the customer at point of purchase. These include building displays, arranging merchandise, decorating windows and stores, sampling customers with new products, etc.

5. *Motivational research*. Studies are devoted to discover why customers buy particular products or services. Alleged and real motives for buying are carefully screened and the results translated into advertising copy and programs, packages, and sales approaches.

6. *Product or brand management*. This is the responsibility of a product or brand manager. Eugene A. Olson, pioneer in brand management, says he manages a brand in contrast to other managers who manage people. The brand manager integrates the work of research and development, production, purchasing, publicity, finance, sales, etc., of one brand or product.

7. *Sales promotion.* This includes "activities that supplement," according to American Marketing Association, "both personal selling and merchandising and coordinate them and help to make them effective"; such as preparing point-of-purchase displays, supplying dealers with premiums or coupons, training dealer-salesmen, arranging tie-in promotions with other companies (paper towels with soap, or carpentry tools with lubrication oil, for example), supplying dealer aids, arranging dealer or customer contests and prizes, etc.

Skills basic to all marketers

Now certain skills and information are valuable to specialists in all the divisions. Whether you remain a salesman or become a sales supervisor, division sales manager, product manager, or advertising man—you need excellent communication skills, studious habits, and cultural appreciations. The road to competence in marketing is an exciting one; you never can completely master it. But you can get better and better. To do so, you'll have to study—to keep abreast of the constant changes going on in marketing.

You can study in two ways: on your own, through systematic reading or correspondence courses, or through attendance at courses offered by colleges, universities, professional organizations. Whichever way you choose—and you may do both, of course—you'll be a better, a more professional salesman for doing so.

Recently, we conducted some formal discussion groups with advertising and sales executives. The groups were held at Foote, Cone & Belding's Chicago office; also in the Consumer Products Division of the Kimberly-Clark Corporation at Neenah, Wisconsin. These two great organizations are leaders in their respective fields. We asked the executives to suggest fields of study and books to read—for the young man bent upon forging ahead in the great profession of marketer. Here are their conclusions:

I. *English*

The basic objectives of the study of English for those entering and progressing in marketing are:

To read efficiently

To write simply and clearly

To spell correctly

To be informed in the field of literature

A. *To read efficiently*

Because the high-level marketer must read a great deal, efficient reading habits are highly desirable —if not required. Three kinds of reading skills are used daily by many marketers.

1. *Skimming*

Here the accent is on speed. Comprehension of the matter read need not be greater than 80 per cent. For marketers (and those who aspire to be marketing executives) a minimal rate of 350 words a minute is expected; at least double that rate is recommended. For skimming efficiency saves time and allows the marketer to read widely articles, brochures, memos, reports, etc., that do not demand analysis.

2. *Analysis*

When the marketer reads analytically, he is intent upon getting the full meaning. Time taken is of secondary importance. Analysis is the kind of reading the marketer does before he signs a contract, an important letter, reads proof, etc.

3. *Forms other than words*

The well-grounded marketer should be efficient in interpreting graphs, figures, and charts. (Recommended basic reading: *How to Read Better and Faster,* 3d ed., by Norman Lewis, Thomas Y. Crowell Company, New York, 1958.)

B. *To write simply and clearly*
Every letter that goes out on your stationery is an instrument of public relations. When the letter is simply, clearly, and graciously written, the company and the writer are likely to benefit. Each memo, bulletin, and report should also be written with concern for their readership. Many marketers study and apply the principles of basic English, or the Flesch Formula to improve the clarity of their writing. These and similar devices are well worth study. Courses in business English often include them.
(Recommended basic reading: *The Art of Readable Writing,* by Rudolph Flesch, Harper & Brothers, New York, 1949.

C. *To spell correctly*
One study indicates that 95 per cent of all misspellings in business correspondence is traceable to 100 words. Lists of commonly misspelled words should therefore be memorized. All marketers should assume direct responsibility for the spelling above their signatures. This responsibility should not be delegated. Another reason why marketers have a vested interest in standard spelling is their responsibility for proofreading. Only the perfect speller can approve copy and formal company communications.
(Recommended basic reading: *How to Be a Better Speller,* by G. D. McEwen, Thomas Y. Crowell Company, New York, 1953.)

    D. To be informed in the field of literature
    Marketers feel a growing concern about their
    cultural responsibilities. Marketers should be
    conversant with many of the so-called world's
    great books. Some of these, of course, are monu-
    ments of literature in languages other than Eng-
    lish. But the best translations of them are in them-
    selves classics of English literature—Edward Fitz-
    gerald's translation of the *Rubaiyat* of Omar
    Khayyám, for example. In short, you should
    know the best that has been thought and said.
II. *Speech*
Everyone, from the youngest salesman to the head
marketer, should speak to the best of his ability.
Ordinarily, this means in a well-modulated and
persuasive voice, in diction that is clear-cut and
standard, without distracting mannerisms, with platform ease and confidence.
    Among the forms of speech that marketers use
frequently in discharging their duties are:
    Oral reading
    Telephone technique
    Dictation of letters, memos, etc.
    Presiding at meetings
    Leading discussions
    Participating in discussions
    Platform presentations
    Holding interviews
To these eight should be added:
    Analytical listening or the understanding of speech
    All nine of these valuable forms of communica-
tions require practice and coaching to master. Many
useful practical speech courses are available throughout the country, in and outside the universities.

Moreover, organizations such as the Toastmaster Clubs make excellent practice media, as do recording machines.

(Recommended basic reading: *How to Talk Well*, by James F. Bender, McGraw-Hill Book Company, Inc., New York, 1957.)

III. *Mathematics*

Marketers, at all levels, need to be proficient in adding, subtracting, dividing. They should know basic statistics, including the Gaussian curve; the standard deviation; the process of adducing the mean, median, and mode of a distribution; theories of sampling; common fallacies of statistical manipulation, etc.

(Recommended basic study: *An Arithmetic Refresher*, by A. Hoover, Holt, Rinehart and Winston, Inc., New York, 1944.)

(Recommended advanced reading: *How to Lie with Statistics*, W. W. Norton & Company, Inc., New York, 1954; *Statistics: A New Approach*, by W. A. Wallis and Harry V. Roberts, Free Press, Glencoe, Ill., 1956.)

IV. *Economics*

A historical review of economic theories is a good place to begin. The marketer should understand the principles of mercantilism, *laissez-faire*, communism, business cycles, etc. He should be acquainted with the great economists and their contributions, e.g., Adam Smith, James and John Stuart Mill, Thomas Malthus, David Ricardo, Robert Owen, Karl Marx, Friedrich Engels, Thorstein Veblen, Henry George, John Keynes, Schumpeter, and others. Moreover, he should be well grounded in the mathematics of marketing and distribution, how to read a profit and loss statement, pricing, budgeting, and the like.

(Recommended basic reading: *On the History and Method of Economics,* by Frank H. Knight, University of Chicago Press, Chicago, 1956.)

(Recommended advanced reading: *Fluctuations, Growth and Forecasting: The Principles of Dynamic Business Economics,* by G. M. Maisel and R. E. Baldwin, John Wiley & Sons, Inc., New York, 1957.)

V. *Marketing*

As we have seen, the composition of marketing is fast changing. It constantly widens its boundaries to include more than direct selling and advertising. A concept of marketing—that includes an entire business enterprise—is defined by Peter Drucker as "the promotion of a product (or service) from its inception through every step of its evolution and distribution until it reaches the satisfied consumer." Once he masters the main principles of marketing, the marketer may want to specialize. He may choose from the divisions of market research as defined by Ruth Vogel earlier in this chapter.

(Recommended basic reading: *Modern Marketing: Dynamics and Management,* by Harry W. Hepner, McGraw-Hill Book Company, Inc., New York, 1955.)

VI. *Business Organization*

Many of your customers are, or will be, big business. To understand their structures is to provide them with more intelligent service. The marketer, therefore, should be acquainted with many aspects of big business, such as: line and staff organization, span of control, centralization, decentralization, policy-making procedures, communications, personnel administration, and allied subjects.

(Recommended basic reading: *Principles of Business Organization and Operation,* by William R. Spriegel

and E. C. Davies, Prentice-Hall, Inc., Englewood
Cliffs, N.J., 1952.)

VII. *Principles of Advertising*

Although advertising is an integral part of marketing, we give it special emphasis. In many companies,
advertising is directed both to industrial and consumer sales. A big company spends many millions
of dollars annually in all media of advertising. Marketers need concentrated study in advertising. In
1890, the total monies spent on advertising in the
United States is estimated at $100 million. This is
much less than the 1959 billings of any one of the
five largest American advertising agencies. Today,
the total national advertising (American) budget exceeds $12 billion annually. As advertising has grown,
certain principles have evolved. These you need to
master as a marketer. Every marketer, therefore,
should know something about the history of advertising, kinds of advertising, the process of putting
together an advertisement and broadcast production,
departmental organization of an advertising agency,
research service, evaluation techniques.

(Recommended basic reading: *Modern Advertising,*
3d ed., by Harry W. Hepner, McGraw-Hill Book
Company, Inc., New York, 1956.)

VIII. *Art Appreciation*

Art and illustration are so intimately linked with
packaging, with display and point-of-sale materials,
with personalized sales presentations, with visual aids
—that a marketer profits from a background of art
appreciation. You'll find the study of aesthetics both
interesting and profitable. Especially the aspects of
art that apply to the marketer's daily challenges are

profitable. Among these are color as motivation, layout, typography, illustration, package design. (Recommended basic reading: *Art in Everyday Life,* 4th ed., by Harriet Goldstein and Vetta Goldstein, The Macmillan Company, New York, 1955.)

IX. *Psychology*

This subject is making new contributions daily— contributions marketers can use. Therefore, you need to be well grounded in the principles of general psychology, particularly the laws of learning, individual differences, sensory appeals, significant contributions of the main current schools of psychology. (Recommended basic reading: *Psychology,* 5th ed., by R. E. Woodworth, Holt, Rinehart and Winston, Inc., New York, 1947.)

Among the two most valuable advanced courses (or studies) in psychology for the marketer are psychology of salesmanship and human relations.

The courses in the psychology of salesmanship include the latest information dealing with getting attention and arousing desire to buy. It includes the basis of motivational research, subliminal stimulation and learning, research techniques in sales psychology, etc.

(Recommended basic reading: *The New Psychology of Selling,* by Mel Hattwick, McGraw-Hill Book Company, Inc., New York, 1959.)

Human relations stresses getting along with people. The marketer depends upon others to a large extent to achieve worthy professional goals. Getting along with others is therefore of prime importance to him and his company. Not only should you learn the theory of good human relations, but its applications.

Further, you'll want a periodic evaluation of the
effectiveness of your own human relations.
(Recommended advanced reading: *Principles of
Human Relations*, by N. R. F. Maier, John Wiley
& Sons, Inc., New York, 1952.)

X. *Philosophy*

Because marketing thrives best in a philosophy of
free opportunity, because marketing serves a philosophy of free opportunity—you as a marketer should
know the main currents of philosophical thought
from Socrates, Plato, and Aristotle down to James,
Whitehead, Santayana, Dewey, Croce, and others.
A marketer's philosophy should provide him with
sound logic to evaluate significant ideas in proportion, to defend and advance the dignity of the individual in an increasingly complex civilization, to
understand the ideas behind the organizations of
which he is a part.
(Recommended basic reading: *The Story of Philosophy*, by Will Durant, Garden City Books, New
York, 1953.)

XI. *Social Science*

The marketer profits from a thorough introduction,
at least, to the fields of sociology, anthropology, history, and political science (in addition to psychology
and economics, already specified). These expanding
fields of human knowledge—often called the behavioral sciences—have significance for the alert marketer. Many colleges and universities offer courses
in social science—sometimes called "contemporary
civilization"—to integrate the disciplines of the subjects mentioned.
(Recommended basic reading: *Introduction to So-*

cial Science, by George C. Atteberry, et al., The Macmillan Company, New York, 1951.)

XII. *General Science*

Our civilization and business ways depend increasingly upon scientific research—pure and applied. An estimated 4,000 new scientific words creep into our language each year. New products, their manufacture and distribution, spring from our scientific laboratories. As the sciences grow in interdependency, the distinctive marketer derives much use and enjoyment from studying them—especially mathematics, biology, physics, chemistry, geology, astronomy.

General science is an attempt to integrate the pure sciences—as opposed to the behavioral or social sciences. It is a subject for the nonspecialist in science. It broadens the marketer's horizons—helps him to keep abreast of modern, important changes in the world of matter.

(Recommended basic reading: *Science in a Changing World,* by E. J. Cable, Prentice-Hall, Inc., Englewood Cliffs, N.J., 1957.)

These 12 areas of human learning offer a constant source of challenge and growth to you as a marketer. Through formal study or systematic reading they permit you to travel much in the realm of gold. And you are a better and a more valuable person for doing so.

14

Twenty Ways to Improve Your Note Taking

> A man will do well to carry a pencil in his pocket and write down the thoughts of the moment.
>
> FRANCIS BACON

To succeed in salesmanship and marketing you must feed on ideas. One excellent way to get ideas is to keep notes on what you see, hear, and read. If you possess anything less than a photographic memory, you'll find an organized plan for note taking necessary. Your notes provide a rich bank of ideas to draw upon when you have problems to solve. With notes, you ensure against forgetting the idea-values you pick up from what you read—hear—see.

As a professional salesman you'll attend many meetings. Your lively interest in meetings—trade associations, training sessions, sales clubs, conventions—is as sure a sign of your professional growth as any. Isn't it also a sign of the respect you have for ideas—and the enormous value of exchanging ideas?

Uses of notes

Much of the value of such meetings depends upon the ideas you carry away with you. As most of us have vagrant memories, we need to take notes at meetings. For notes— excellent notes—save time, help to develop logical and creative thinking, aid memory, are sources of ideas in compact, easy-to-find form. They are valuable work materials to help promote your job efficiency.

Of course, you'll find other occasions than meetings for note taking. For example, at the end of the day you may want to sum up your calls in note form—what happened when you got or failed to get the order. When you take a course or follow a reading program, you take notes for reference and review.

How to take notes

Analyze excellent notes and you discover they follow certain well-defined principles. And when you apply the principles, you find they make your note taking efficient and easy. With faithful practice, you convert these principles into habits of the profitable sort.

Dr. C. C. Crawford, professor of psychology at the University of Southern California, and other authorities stress 20 basic principles of note taking. Here are those principles in the form of 20 suggestions, many of them adapted from Professor Crawford's excellent book, *How to Study* (now out of print, regrettably).

1. *Begin now a definite system of notes if you have not already done so.* The need for planning your note-taking system—instead of just letting it grow like Topsy—is well demonstrated by a study conducted at Carnegie Institute of

Technology. Some years ago that distinguished center of learning appointed a committee to investigate note-taking problems of executives. Here are some of the interesting results:

a. All executives reported the need for taking and keeping notes.

b. Most of the executives said that whatever system they used developed out of trial and error.

c. All the executives recommended that a streamlined system of note taking be taught in high schools and colleges—one that includes outlining.

d. Seventy-five per cent of the executives reported that they changed their ways of taking notes over the years. They gradually improved them by trial and error.

e. All of the executives named the worst note-taking sin as "writing notes on scraps of paper that soon became lost or misplaced."

f. A majority of the executives learned to keep important notes in a file or loose-leaf binder.

g. Some of the executives have their secretaries type the notes shortly after they are made.

2. *Use a loose-leaf notebook.*

a. You can organize all valuable notes into a uniform system.

b. For this you'll find a loose-leaf form absolutely essential. Otherwise you can't place later material on a given topic with that which came in earlier.

c. A loose-leaf system saves time and paper—is compact. You can use every sheet.

d. It permits you to carry notes on all important subjects in one binder.

e. You can revise one page without spoiling the whole book. It saves you unnecessary copying.

f. A loose-leaf system helps you to reclassify easily so you can bring all material on a given subject together. You simply rearrange the sheets. Suppose, for example, in your pursuit of creative selling over the next two or three years—you stress at various times such topics as buying psychology, impulse buying, buyers' prejudices. At the end of the two- or three-year period, you may want to sort out the papers that cover these topics and combine them under a main heading, such as "The Mind of the Buyer." The loose-leaf system permits you to do this.

Or suppose you need to prepare a speech on creative selling. You go through your notes, you take out the pages that deal with that subject, you assemble them, you cull them for ideas. Presto! You have all your ideas at your finger-tips. The loose-leaf system permits you to do this.

3. *Use a large-size notebook.* A pocket-size notebook sooner or later gives you trouble. Eventually you almost always abandon it. (We're talking about a place for *permanent* notes.) The pocket-size notebook cramps your style— it gets filled up too soon. It forces you to put material on several sheets which would have more meaning presented to your eyes all at once.

On the other hand, the large notebook serves you as a writing desk. You can also often use it as a temporary file. For example, suppose you wanted to retain an outline of some notes on a *Sales Management* tear-sheet article. You read it. You punched three holes in it—because you wanted to take notes on it later. You inserted it in your ring binder. Then some evening shortly after, you took notes on it and substituted the notes for the article.

4. *Plan a filing system along with your note-taking system.* When you take good notes you have won only half the battle; the other half is to make them easy to find. A collection of notes taken without thought for the future can

scarcely be so arranged or classified as to be of ready service later. When your collection is small, you may be able to find what you want without too much trouble. But after you've amassed a lot of notes over the years, you'll be in hot water—unless you have followed a system of classification, indexing, and orderly arrangement. (See pages 64–67.)

Organize your notes as you go along. A salesman we know follows the profitable pursuit of revising his notebook once a week. Sometimes this takes him a few minutes. One Sunday morning, for example, he spent three-quarters of an hour inserting and indexing notes.

As your binder of notes grows, the day will come when you have to discard some of the pages. When this happens you'll have to make a choice: throw away or file them. Ordinarily, if you found them valuable enough to write up, you'll want to keep them. In that event, file them in Manila folders, each labeled according to the subject, or file them in a cabinet or drawer.

5. *Adopt a fairly small unit.* Basic questions: How much to put on a page, when to stop, and when to start a new page?

One suggestion: Put on one sheet if possible—one or both sides—the notes of an entire speech, article, or chapter. Always be careful to start another speech, article, or chapter on a new page.

Otherwise, if you start a second subject (speech or article) on the same page, you lose the prime purpose of the loose-leaf system—ready classification.

6. *Give each page of notes a close heading to show its source and its subject.* For example:

"Creative Selling," speech by Alex Osborn, Hotel Roosevelt, N. Y. 4/24/53.

The reason for this suggestion, of course, is this: Since the various pages may later be separated, you have to identify each page. A common error, for example, is this: In taking notes on a book, such as *Creative Imagination* by Alex Osborn, to label a note page "Chapter 11" but omit the reference to the book and author.

7. *Assign to each note a number or letter to represent its status in the outline.* (Here, you see, we are getting into outlining.) You should adopt a system of notation symbols and adhere to it. Here's a common useful one:

I.
  A.
    1.
      a.
        (1)
          (*a*)

The system is simple. You alternate numbers and letters.

8. *Use generous indentations.* The chief virtue of generous indentations is that they give you a quick visual impression of the outline—or bony structure.

You often see two common "boo-boos" in indentation: One is failure to indent enough: the other is indenting so far that most of the notes are written on very short lines on the right side of the page—and the greater part of the page is then blank.

9. *Indent overrun lines slightly more than the beginnings of the first lines.* To illustrate:

Wrong

a. This is a sample of overrun lines; they are not properly indented.

Right

a. This is a sample of overrun lines.
   They are properly indented.

10. *Leave reasonably wide margins.* If your notes are in good shape, you leave a fairly wide margin at the top and left, lesser margins at the right.

You'll find the left margin is particularly useful if you want to use it later for revisions. The top is essential for the later addition of index headings, etc.

11. *Avoid writing notes in long paragraphs.* Notes should always be in outline form. A paragraph of notes containing, say, 100 words represents two note-taking errors. Either it covers several points, each of which you should have written separately, or you wrote too much. If you need more than two lines to state your point, you probably are committing one or the other of these two errors.

12. *Take notes in quotation form only for special purposes.* Otherwise state the idea in your own words. Remember, quotations apart from their context don't ordinarily mean as much to you as your own words. Too, it takes longer to write quotations than your summary of them. As you grow in note-taking ability, you develop facility in boiling down—in succinctness.

13. *State points briefly and concisely.* Good notes are brief, to the point, yet at the same time clear and meaningful. If your notes—your sentences or phrases—are too long, you sacrifice organization. Also, if you're taking notes on a speech, you miss too much, you don't have time to listen.

Of course, you'll have to develop selectivity. You'll want to take down in greater detail than usual:

  a. The unfamiliar
  b. The different
  c. Key facts
  d. Things you'll use after long periods of time
  f. Things not available elsewhere
  g. Quotations or figures that are useless unless complete and accurate

Condense all other materials as much as possible. Why not use this standard measure? Write your notes fully enough so that another person would have no trouble understanding their meaning. You then will be certain to understand them.

14. *Study and practice the boiling-down technique.* Here are some helpful hints to develop this valuable skill:

a. Read or listen until you understand the point before you write it down.

b. Classify points into groups and with each one eliminate unnecessary words or repetition.

c. State the point instead of merely naming it; statements always convey more thought per word than topics.

d. Omit unnecessary words even at the expense of grammar. Use dashes and other punctuation marks.

e. Use abbreviations for long words: Sm (supermarket), psy (psychology), HO (home office), CS (creative selling), etc.

f. Look for the summary or topic sentence. It bears the main idea of the paragraph.

g. Use key words to help you remember the points.

15. *Get the points down in their logical relationship.* This is one of the chief reasons for outlining. Organized notes are always more valuable and coherent than a mere list of jottings.

In outlining an article, for example, you may save time in the long run by skimming it first.

Then, when you actually outline the article in note form, you'll have a well-knit, concise piece of work. May we suggest here, too, that you make use of transition words and phrases, such as:

a. In the second (2nd) place

b. Again

c. Thirdly (or 3rd or 3)

d. On the other hand

These are signposts—enumerators.

16. *Practice to increase your speed of note taking.* The more you work at it—the easier it becomes—the more proficient you become.

Incidentally, the faster you read, the easier your note taking on books and articles becomes. (Those who find that they read slowly may speed up with coaching.)

17. *Take notes in the best form possible and revise, if necessary, later on.* In the beginning you may feel the need of revising your notes before you commit them to your binder.

Eventually, however, you'll become such an excellent note taker that you'll be able to set down your notes immediately in your loose-leaf binder in final form.

18. *Don't use shorthand.* We mention this even though most of us don't know shorthand. How often do we hear "If I had only studied shorthand, note taking would be a cinch."

Learning shorthand is expensive. If you don't use it constantly, you forget it. Those who take notes in shorthand ordinarily take down too much. Often, unless shorthand notes are transcribed, you can't read them years later. It actually is hard to find the main points in a mass of shorthand notes. Note takers who use shorthand are usually poor outliners. Studies prove this. Finally, shorthand note taking actually discourages intelligent listening and creative reading.

19. *Develop your own short cuts.* Many of us who write slowly have our own system of abbreviation.

One system is Speedwriting. In this system we write words without their vowels. For example: "Nw s th tm to tk gd nts." You may ask "Isn't this a form of shorthand?" No. Because almost anyone can read it who hasn't studied it. Use other short cuts, as *W* for "with," drop articles— "the," "a." Use arrows and dashes as substitutes for verbs.

In all such recommendations bear this in mind: Use anything that works—that's understandable.

20. *Hold the right attitude toward note taking.*

a. Have a strong purpose to remember what you write down. It will stay with you longer.

b. Thoroughly understand and master the idea before you write it down.

c. Develop, through practice, the ability to write one thought as you listen to another.

d. Make your note taking thoughtful rather than mechanical.

e. Review all your notes at least once before you file them. Make corrections if necessary.

f. Exercise judgment. Write down some things; trust your memory for other things. Notes should be so written as to stimulate and revive memories. Remember, the psychologists tell us we never forget anything. We only repress memories. Good notes help us to break through our repressions. They thus unlock the mighty storehouse of our memories.

Jules B. Singer, marketing consultant, in a recent article in *Sales Meetings* lists six useful functions of note taking—particularly at sales meetings:

1. The audience pays closer attention.
2. It gets involved to a greater degree with the speaker and speech.
3. It translates the speaker's thoughts into its own words.
4. Listeners can stress points for follow-up.
5. The speaker has the opportunity to emphasize and dramatize important points.
6. The audience is more likely to refer back to its own notes.

15

How to Write Excellent Letters, Reports, and Memos—Easily

> The difference between the right word and the almost right word is the difference between lightning and the lightning bug.
>
> MARK TWAIN

If you are like most salesmen, you hate to write letters. reports, and memos. You find them a galling chore. Somehow you feel stymied every time you have to put your thoughts on paper. You wouldn't begrudge the time they take if you could make them read as fluently as you talk.

Even so, you do want to write excellent letters, reports, and memos. You know you must write them if you are to do your job well. You know that higher responsibilities entail facility in writing—as well as speaking. You know that simple, direct writing is a valuable tool for salesmen to have and use. You'll want to make your letters, reports, and memos your faithful ambassadors. When you let them represent you and your company as they should, you're the winner!

188

Perhaps you've found yourself in the predicament of the salesman who recently said: "I'm about four months behind in writing reports on my promotions. And I've got a stack of letters to answer. If I could learn a few tricks of the writer's trade, I'd be happier—and further along. At this stage, writing's the only thing I don't like about my job."

Let's assume that you are in a state similar to that of the salesman just quoted. What to do? Here are five suggestions:

1. Stop suggesting to yourself that writing is difficult for you.

2. Suggest to yourself, "I can learn to write as readily as I learned to talk."

3. Do the exercises and assignments in this chapter. You'll find them easy to do.

4. Promise yourself you'll put to practice, every time you write, the four basic skills you'll learn in this chapter. Stay with them until they are fast habits.

5. Enter upon your writing duties from now on with zest. Think of each of your letters, reports, memos as a building block in your edifice of success.

If you'll follow those five suggestions, you'll improve mightily your letters, reports, and memos and make writing a painless and interesting task.

Of course, you won't expect to become a Shakespeare in four lessons. (Who today wants to write business letters in Shakespeare's style anyway!)

But you can expect to improve your writing in many specific ways. Result, you'll save a lot of time to spend on more sales calls, more hours with your family, more rest or recreation. Moreover, you'll break down that frustrated feeling that comes on every time you write. And you won't hesitate to write as you talk.

The main idea behind the four basic skills is to do just that—*write as you talk* (provided you talk well).

In other words, your goal now is to "write as you would talk to your reader in easy, pleasant conversation." Why? Because that kind of writing is the easiest to read—also the easiest to write, once you master the four basic skills. It's the kind of writing to help you do your job more easily and better—the kind to quicken your efficiency and advancement.

Back in 1921, Prof. Harry D. Kitson of Columbia University wrote a book, *Advertising*. In this book he pioneered in presenting "readability statistics." Ever since, the psychologists have followed through with studies and experiments in this field. Result: We have the key to make writing easy to read, and also to learn to write easily.

Among the other leaders in simplified, successful writing today are Dr. Edgar Dale, Dr. Rudolph Flesch, Prof. Irving Lorge. We shall make use of their research and discoveries. Of these three distinguished psychologists, the writings of Dr. Rudolph Flesch are perhaps most popularly known.

How to write short sentences that sell

The magic key to successful letters, reports, and memos is simplicity. One excellent way to simplicity is through short sentences.

Short sentences save you time. They help you say what you mean and mean what you say. Therefore, they help you think straight and fast. And never forget: Short sentences save your reader time. They give him a sense of achievement because he understands them easily. He'll be grateful to you for writing short sentences.

Keep in mind from now on—whenever you write:

1. Short sentences are easy to read.

2. Short sentences are easy to write.
3. Short sentences are easy to dictate.
4. Short sentences are short cuts to clear thinking.
5. Short sentences are persuasive: they help you sell.

Refer to the *Table of Reading Ease*—based on Dr. Flesch's research—until you memorize it:

	Table of Reading Ease	
Average number of words in sentence		*Description of style*
1–8	....	Very easy
9–11	....	Easy
12–14	....	Fairly easy
15–17	....	Standard
18–21	....	Fairly difficult
22–25	....	Difficult
26 (and more)	....	Very difficult

Assignment

After each of the sentences in the memorandum below, write the word (or words) that describes its length. (Refer to the *Table of Reading Ease* above.) For example, "Most business letters are too long." (very easy)

(1) Often you read business letters that ramble all over which is a bad thing for them to do because in that way they often confuse the reader, and make him reread it or parts of it. (_____) (2) Whether he is conscious of it or not, the reader is actually grateful for conciseness. (_____) (3) It helps to make his workday shorter and easier. (_____) (4) So make your business letters short. (_____)

Your fill-in words for the four sentences above should be (1) very difficult; (2) standard; (3) easy; (4) very easy.

If your answers don't agree, recount and refer to the *Table of Reading Ease*. Continue in the same way with the following sentences.

1. Over a period of years many of our salesmen have requested a course in business correspondence. (_____)

2. This course was finally prepared in response to the requests received from these salesmen and I am not at all hesitant in recommending it without reservation. (_____)

3. I believe that every man who wishes to get ahead in the business world should learn how to write excellent letters, reports, and memoranda. (_____)

4. Words, sentences, and paragraphs are tools of selling, management, and personal success. (_____)

5. Next to good speech, I know of nothing more basic to a man's success in business and industry than an easy ability to write or dictate a first-class letter, report, or memorandum. (_____)

6. I therefore urge you to take every possible advantage of this course in business correspondence. (_____)

7. The time you spend on this course is an investment in your own future which will pay dividends for the rest of your business career. (_____)

8. The time required is approximately two hours per month. (_____)

9. The young men in our organization should especially welcome this opportunity to improve themselves. (_____)

10. All men and women in our company, however, will benefit from this course. (_____)

11. But your benefits will only be in direct proportion to the efforts you expend. (_____)

Correct answers are given upside down.

(1) standard; (2) very difficult; (3) difficult; (4) fairly easy; (5) very difficult; (6) standard; (7) difficult; (8) easy; (9) fairly easy; (10) fairly easy; (11) fairly easy.

Most letters, reports, and memos have a number of sentences. Ordinarily the sentences vary in length. How can you estimate the readability of an entire letter, report, or memo?

Simply find the average. Total the words of all the sentences. Then divide by the number of sentences. For example, the 11 numbered sentences above contain 202 words. Divide the number of words by the number of sentences and you get 18 plus. The average sentence length, then, is about 18 words. That makes the sentence style of the writing *fairly difficult* to read. Define a "sentence" as any unit of thought that ends with a period, question mark, or exclamation point.

Semicolon. Example:

The plan is practical; you'll like it.

Colon. Example:

Result: We had a successful meeting.

Dash. Example:

The sales manager—armed with reports—was prepared.

Parenthesis. Example:

The hard-working salesman (he worked from early morning to late at night) made a lot of money.

Quotation Marks. Example:

The buyer called in his secretary and said, "Please take this memo."

There are exceptions to these rules, but you don't need to learn them now. They apply mostly to dialogue writing.

Assignment

Write a memo to your boss. Describe the training in writing you're giving yourself. Make your average sentence length 14 or fewer words. Write no sentence longer than 17 words (standard). Feel free to vary the length of your sentences, but keep them short. Their average length should make your memo fairly easy reading at least.

Go through your files and select a copy of one of your

sales reports, letters, or memos. The one you select should be at least 150 words long. Now rewrite it in a fairly easy sentence length.

Suggestions

1. From now on write short sentences.

2. Estimate the readability of books, newspapers, and magazines you read. Several times a day count the sentence length of a paragraph or two. This will help to make you sentence-length conscious. Before long you'll have the habit of writing short, clear sentences without having to count words.

3. Whenever possible edit your writing—for sentence length—before you commit it to final form.

How to streamline your written words

The world's great salesmen use short, simple words. They want to reach the most hearts and minds. To do this, they speak and write the common man's language. For instance:

1. "The only way I know to solve problems between people is through talk."—ERNST MAHLER

2. "Aim high; think in terms of big money."—THOMAS J. WATSON

3. "If an army travels on its stomach, a sales force travels on its heart."—WILLIAM J. FRENCH

4. "A great salesman can make as well as fire shots."—L. E. PHENNER

5. "What we need in salesmen is more composers and fewer musicians."—AL. N. SEARES

6. "You can't buy money with happiness."—ROBERT J. KORETZ

Notice: The six sentences have sixty-two words. Forty-six of the words have one syllable; thirteen of the words have two syllables; only three of the words have more than two syllables.

Assignment

Write a simpler word that means the same (or nearly the same) as each of the following:

1. illumination _____
2. primary _____
3. parsimonious _____
4. inclement _____
5. commensurate _____
6. acrimonious _____
7. ludicrous _____
8. physiognomy _____
9. imprecation _____
10. iniquitous _____

How do your words compare with those given upside down?

(1) light; (2) first; (3) stingy; (4) harsh; (5) equal; (6) bitter; (7) funny; (8) face; (9) curse; (10) wicked.

How to test your word ease

Do your letters, reports, and memos have more than 175 syllables to every 100 words? If so, you are using too many big words for mass appeal. Memorize the following table of word ease.

Syllables per 100 words	Description of style
150 (or fewer)	Very easy
151–160	Easy
161–170	Fairly easy
171–175	Standard
176–180	Fairly difficult
181–190	Difficult
191 (and above)	Very difficult

Webster states that a syllable is: "in writing, a part of a word separated, as at the end of a line, from the rest of the word." Examples: *let-ter par-a-graph.* (If you have difficulty in dividing words into syllables, a dictionary indicates syllables.)

Assignment

How many syllables does each of the following words have?

1. salesmanship _____
2. advertising _____
3. creativity _____
4. commission _____
5. business _____
6. merchandising _____
7. mileage _____
8. quarterly _____
9. promotion _____
10. gondola _____

Check your answers with those given upside down:

(1) 3; (2) 4; (3) 5; (4) 3; (5) 2; (6) 4; (7) 2; (8) 3; (9) 3; (10) 3.

Assignment

At the end of each sentence below, write the word (or words, that describes (*a*) its sentence-length style and (*b*) its word ease.

1. It is possible that we had more than the average personal interest in this point, because, as previously made known to you, the bulk of the goods sold indirectly to the Smith Company is distributed in Joe Smith's territory, and we are not at all pleased with the way that things are going on at this moment.

(*a*. _____)
(*b*. _____)

2. The buyers that I have talked to about this bonus

aren't excited about it because they all say that they got "stuck" on the last offer.

(*a.* _____)
(*b.* _____)

3. Since such information has been given, I informed Chicago that it would be satisfactory with practically all of my accounts, the names of which I submitted and amongst those were Smith Company, to automatically include 5 or 10 cases of merchandise in such carload shipments.

(*a.* _____)
(*b.* _____)

4. My purpose in writing you regarding the subject matter is to forcefully bring to your attention the importance of securing your transportation tickets well in advance of the scheduled meeting.

(*a.* _____)
(*b.* _____)

5. The attitude of our customers and the extent of their merchandising activity on our line indicated very excellent handling by the salesmen and the division manager formerly responsible for that area.

(*a.* _____)
(*b.* _____)

Check your answers with those given upside down:

(1. *a*) very difficult; (1. *b*) very easy; (2. *a*) very difficult; (2. *b*) very easy; (3. *a*) very difficult; (3. *b*) very easy; (4. *a*) very difficult; (4. *b*) very easy; (5. *a*) very difficult; (5. *b*) very difficult.

Assignment

1. How many words in the following memo? _____
2. What is the style of its sentence length? _____
3. How many syllables in the following memo? _____

4. What is its word ease? _____

5. Rewrite the memo in a *very easy* style both in sentence length and word ease.

Since the initiation of our new expense report program, most of our salesmen have responded in a remarkably distinguished manner. Nevertheless, we are still the recipients of many reports, notable for their incorrectness. A goodly number of the erroneous entries pertain to the total which are faultily extended on the bottom and side of the report. Many salesmen are neglecting to follow the directions implicitly. Every instance of incorrectly made out expense reports results in unnecessary procrastination and burdensome labor at the home office. Your complete cooperation in reviewing the procedure of filling out the expense report is earnestly solicited.

The style of sentence length and word ease are printed upside down:

sentence-length style is standard; word ease is difficult.

Assignment

After you have completed the assignment above go through your file. Select several of your carbon copies of letters, reports, or memos. Estimate their word ease. Rewrite them in a *very easy, easy, fairly easy* or *standard* style —whichever you select before rewriting.

From now on, watch that word! Select simple words before you write the final draft of your letters, reports, or memos.

One idea to a paragraph

Let's turn to the paragraph. Webster says a paragraph is "a distinct section or subdivision of a letter . . . whether it has one or many sentences, the paragraph is a unit that deals with a particular point."

The ideal paragraph for a business letter, report, or memo (1) is short; (2) contains one main point.

For example:

10/1/61

Dear Joe,

Let me tell you about the new promotions in my territory.

You'll be glad to know that four customers are planning promotions. These are Continental Divide Drug; P&A Food Stores; GIA Cooperatives; Great Outlets.

Continental Divide Drug likes our personally conducted point-of-purchase handouts.

P&A stores will run R.O.P. ads featuring our full line.

GIA Cooperatives are talking about a combination offer.

Great Outlets are going to mass-display our products in all the windows.

You may be sure of two things: I'll keep you informed of progress; I'll stay enthusiastic about the way things are going.

Best regards,
Alex

Now note this: The sample letter has seven short paragraphs. Paragraph 1 tells what the subject of the letter is. Paragraph 2 specifies four customers planning promotions. Paragraphs 3, 4, 5, 6 each takes up a different customer's promotion. Paragraph 7 makes two gracious promises.

Assignment

Rewrite the following letter in paragraphs. We'll number the sentences for reference later on.

Dear Joe:

(1) You'll be interested to know I'm trying to improve my writing. (2) I'm reading a book on Basic English by I. A. Richards. (3) Basic English is designed to simplify correspondence. (4) It is composed of 850 of the most often used words in the English language. (5) All 850 words are printed on one side of an 8½- by 11-inch page. (6) Basic English is now used widely. (7) The English foreign office uses it in correspondence with its dependencies. (8) Shakespeare, Dickens, and other classic authors are translated into Basic English. (9) The Russians are teaching their high school students Basic English. (10) I find that it has much to offer a fellow like me—although I haven't mastered it yet. (11) It will help me to write more simply. (12) I find the 850 words cover most of my language needs —except for brand names. (13) But Basic English lets us add brand names—and technical words too—to the 850. (14) I hope you'll notice improvement in my letters and reports—once I master Basic English.

Warm regards,
Alex

Read upside down:

The letter breaks down logically into five paragraphs: Paragraph 1. Sentences 1, 2 announce the subject. Paragraph 2. Sentences 3, 4, 5 define Basic English. Paragraph 3. Sentences 6, 7, 8, 9 describe uses of Basic English. Paragraph 4. Sentences 10, 11, 12, 13 tell how Basic English meets Alex's needs. Paragraph 5. Sentence 14 expresses Alex's hope for improvement.

As another exercise in correct paragraph writing, write a letter, report, or memo to your boss about what you're doing to improve yourself.

1. Write short sentences.
2. Use simple words.
3. Put one main point in each paragraph.

Make your letters and memos conversational

As you read through the letters you receive, notice the variety of styles. Some are warm, direct—just as if the writer were chatting with you. Others are stiff and formal as all get out.

Notice for example, this opening sentence: "It is to be wished that all weekly reports be mailed each Friday." Why not "Please mail your weekly reports on Fridays"? The second sentence has half the words of the first; is a courteous order; has "your" in it. It reads better, and you like it better.

To make your style conversational, follow these ten simple rules. You'll find all of them easy to apply.

1. *Use "you," "we," "I," and the other personal pronouns.* Sales consultant Zenn Kaufman tells this story: "When the time came for Al Smith to write his memoirs, every big syndicate in America was angling for the rights. McNaught Syndicate won the prize, and on the basis of a guarantee that was not as high as some of the other bids. When asked how McNaught got this lucky break, Smith said, 'It's very simple. All the others told me how important they were. McNaught told me how important *I* was.' " Letters, like selling, benefit from the personal approach.

Of all 10 rules this one is the most basic. Here are some examples:

Impersonal	*Personal*
1. It would be helpful if a joint call could be made on the buyer.	If *you* and *I* make a joint call on the buyer, we could help *him* and *ourselves*.

Impersonal	*Personal*
2. It is pleasant to report—	*You'll* be pleased to know—
3. There should be two sales-men to help at the convention.	*You* may want to send two salesmen—like Jim Smith and Tom Brown—to help *me* at the convention.
4. Here is a report on territory # 10.	*You'll* find *my* report on territory # 10 enclosed.
5. No confirmation of the order has been received.	*We* haven't received a confirmation of the order.

You'll perk up the reader's interest by using his name occasionally throughout the letter—especially if it's long. For example, suppose in the third paragraph you write, "You'll also be interested, John, in last week's sales." Just as we like to hear our name, so do we like to see it.

2. *Use contractions.* Modern business correspondence is much less formal than formerly. Most firms permit and encourage their salesmen—and other employees—to write conversationally. A good way to do this is to use common contractions. For example:

you'll	for	you will
we'll	for	we will
I'm	for	I am
you're	for	you are
can't	for	cannot
aren't	for	are not
won't	for	will not
doesn't	for	does not
they're	for	they are

3. *Use active voice, not passive voice.*

Passive voice	*Active voice*
No bill has been received by us.	We haven't received your bill.
It was understood that the steel girders would be shipped.	We understood that the....
A quarter a case was lost by	The buyer lost a quarter a

Passive voice	*Active voice*
the buyer because of the late arrival of the merchandise.	case. The merchandise arrived late.

4. *Use simple rather than complex sentences.* (This means sometimes you have to break up a complex sentence into more than one simple sentence.) For example:

Complex sentences	*Simple sentences*
Your bill, which is detailed but does not allow the usual 2 per cent discount, needs correction.	Please revise your bill to allow the usual 2 per cent discount.
This territory, that has long been neglected, needs a lot of work.	This territory has long been neglected. It needs a lot of work.
The buyer, for whom I have a lot of respect, has a justifiable complaint.	The buyer has a justifiable complaint. I have a lot of respect for him.

5. *Use everyday words, not bookish words.* For example:

Everyday words	*Bookish words*
go to bed	retire
get up	arise
keep	retain
legs	limbs
dress	clothe
pick	select
make a speech	deliver an oration
light	illumination
letter	communication

6. *Avoid worn-out, old-fashioned expressions.*

Old-fashioned	*Modern*
In reply wish to state ...	May I say ...
This is to advise you ...	You'll be interested to know ...
Even date ...	Today ...

Old-fashioned	Modern
In compliance with your request...	We grant your request...
Your letter of Sept. 14 has just come to hand...	I've just received your Sept. 14th letter...
In reference to your communication of...	Thank you for your letter of...

7. Use direct, not roundabout, expressions.

Roundabout	Direct
in case of	if
as a result of	because
in addition	also
with the result that	so that
prior to	before
in the event that	if
at the present time	now

8. Use friendly, not formal, words.

Formal	Friendly
assistance	help
manner	way
unable to effect alteration	can't change
the writer	I, we, he
telephone (verb)	call (verb)
regret most sincerely	am sorry

9. Avoid present participles.

Present participles	Substitutes
Confirming our conversation of...	May I confirm...
Replying to your letter of...	Thank you for your letter of...
Complying with your request...	I'm happy to comply with...
While calling on Mr. Jones...	When I called on Mr. Jones...

Present participles	Substitutes
When talking with Mr. Smith on Monday...	I talked with Mr. Smith on Monday...

10. *Use a bit of slang if you're writing to a friend or an acquaintance.* Carl Sandburg says, "Slang is a language that rolls up its sleeves, spits on its hands, and goes to work." But make sure the reader understands the slang.

Slang	Formal
Is my face red!	I am deeply embarrassed.
To get the hang of it	To understand it
Mad, teed off	Angry
Happy landings!	May it turn out well.
Cheerio!	Cheerful greetings.

You'll use rule 10 with your common sense and good taste. Remember also, you occasionally should break a rule —but only for a purpose.

Every time you receive a well-written letter, study it. Which of the 10 rules does the writer use? What other tricks of the writer's trade did he use to make you like his style? Through this approach you'll learn much more than this short chapter can give you.

Here's an exercise to test your ability to write a letter in conversational style.

Assignment

Rewrite the following letter:

Dear Mr. White,

The recent letter sent to Mr. John Jones, sales manager of XYZ Company, has just come to hand. That there has been some apparent neglect of my customers is well taken.

During the last two weeks I have been suffering from bursitis at home, thus making sales calls impossible.

I shall make it my business to call next week, offering

my apologies and hoping to explain the whole matter satisfactorily.

                          Very truly yours,
                          John Tate

Here's a rewrite. It includes the recommendations in this chapter. How does it compare with your rewrite?

Dear Mr. White,
    Mr. John Jones, my sales manager, gave me your recent letter to answer. I apologize for not calling on you in the last three weeks. Certainly, you have every reason to feel neglected.
    You see, Mr. White, I've been home with a painful shoulder. The doctor calls it bursitis. That's why I couldn't call on you or any of my other customers.
    Please forgive me. I hope to be fit by next week. I shall call on you first. Let's hope I can make up to you—in good measure—for the inconvenience I've caused you and Smith Bros., Inc.

                          Faithfully yours,
                          John Tate

Assignment

Pick five of your own letters from carbon copies in your files. Study them in light of the suggestions given in this chapter. Rewrite them if they aren't conversational in style. If you haven't any copies, write a letter to the personnel manager of a company. Apply for a position in the company. Write the letter in conversational style. How many of the 10 simple rules given above did you include?

16

Eighteen Ways to Create Ideas for Sales Presentations and Promotions

> Creativity is but a pair of fresh eyes.
>
> FAIRFAX M. CONE

Like the advertising man, the professional salesman builds sales and good will with novel ideas. He practices *creative thinking*. The phrase frightens many, yet it needn't. For creative thinking is within normal capabilities. According to psychologist William Easton, "The creative thinker evolves no new ideas. He actually evolves new combinations of ideas that are already in his mind." This comforting thought is a good one to hold on to when we start a program of creating ideas.

Until the salesman realizes his constant need for promotional ideas and sets up some system of producing them, he can scarcely lay claim to purposiveness. "Ideas are like beards," said Voltaire. "Men do not have them until they grow up." Rather than wait for the occasionally inspired idea, the professional salesman uses well-defined techniques regularly—techniques and exercises to produce ideas to increase his sales and service, to enrich his career. Let's review those he may use often.

1. *Think of analogies.* Christopher Sholes, inventor of the typewriter, couldn't arrange its keyboard until he thought of the manuals of an organ. The inventor of the spray carburetor was stymied until he saw his wife use a perfume atomizer. A salesman of paper tissues sneezed at a soda bar. Why not a "Sneezin' Season Bar"? This idea led to a most successful country-wide promotion of his products tied in with cold remedies.

The professional salesman knows that analogies are numberless. His chief challenge is to make a habit of looking and listening for them.

2. *Make free association work.* Suppose you wanted to explore your reactions to the word "service." You might then say, "I'm going to write during the next two minutes (as fast and uncritically as I can) all the words that 'service' and the successive associations stimulate. Here's what I get as I do that simple exercise. *Service: help, good, need, want, people, do, serve, like, pay, growing, gratitude, thanks, more, competition, beat, give, increase . . .*"

Take the name of one of your products. See how many associations you can write down in two or three minutes. You may find a new talking point or two in your list. Such an exercise points to the marvelous fecundity of the human mind—the human mind that's never idle, always ready with a flow of ideas. Salesmen who use this association exercise say they derive at least three benefits from it. They gain confidence in their infinite capacity to think creatively; they get ideas to use in their work; they develop the habit to use associations throughout the day. For example, a salesman read an article as he waited in a buyer's outer office—about the china collection in the White House. He jotted down a memo to his sales promotion manager: "Why not replicas of the White House china collection as premiums? See *National Geographic Magazine*, January issue, 1961."

3. *Make new patterns*. The 26 letters of the English alphabet, combined in various patterns, give us a vocabulary of more than a million words! Notice how the substitution of one phonetic sound in "Little children should be seen and not heard," produced an excellent slogan for National Safety Council: "Little children should be seen and not hurt." At a recent bartenders' convention, more than 2,000 recipes for new cocktails were submitted—new combinations of basic liquors.

In how many different patterns can you arrange these three lines of equal length _____ _____ _____? One salesman constructed 13 different patterns from them in three minutes, used some of the patterns as models when he built displays for point-of-sale merchandising.

4. *Take an idea inventory*. Have you ever read a book entitled *Cookery in the Middle Ages?* Probably not, since there's no such title in the U.S. Catalogue. However, you can ask hundreds of questions about cookery in the middle ages. In three minutes, if you wished, you could write 10 or more questions, such as:

How did they serve the food?
What vegetables did they have?
What spices did they use for seasoning?
Did they know anything about a balanced diet?
Did they eat three times a day?
How did they preserve food for winter?
What were their table manners like?
Did they use forks?
How did they prepare for a banquet?

What kinds of utensils did they have?

(How many more questions can you jot down in three minutes?)

Now let's suppose you were offered a dollar for each question you could write about cookery in the Middle Ages. Could you write a thousand or more of them? Of course.

Suppose you've written many questions about a subject. The next step would be to classify them in logical groups according to subject matter. Then you could do some research to find answers to them. Result would be enough information to write a book. Each group of questions— and their answers—might make a chapter.

The point is, we can ask questions about subjects of which we know little or nothing. Professional salesmen use this technique of asking questions. Suppose, for example, you're a new salesman, calling on supermarket buyers. You could write an idea inventory on "What I'd Like to Know about Supermarket Management." A hundred or more questions on that subject would help you in many ways— to get specific information, to help you talk the buyer's language, to give you ideas for sales promotions, etc.

Or suppose you wrote questions about "My Ten Toughest on-the-job Problems." Wouldn't they guide you to the answers? The idea inventory or self-quiz technique is an excellent way to creative thinking.

5. *Use deep analysis.* A famous advertising man retired to a ranch in the Southwest. He sympathized with his neighbors, a tribe of impoverished Navajo shepherds. He wanted to help them help themselves. He said to himself, "How can I use my advertising know-how and the wool from the Navajos' flocks—to help the Indians and occupy my spare time?" After weeks of intensive thinking he came up with a possibility: Why not ask the Indians to weave some plaid woolen ties? Why not sell them by mail? He did this on a

trial basis. Eventually, he built a million-dollar-a-year business selling Navajo-woven ties to men (and women) by mail.

Rex Stout used deep analysis, as we've seen in Chapter 2, to find a solution to his problem.

Suppose you had an appointment for just ten minutes in which to make a sales presentation to an important prospect —one who never had time to see you before. What would you include in your sales presentation? Before preparing it you would analyze his needs, his interests, his present source of supply, your competitors' prices and services, the services and product advantages you and your company could provide him, etc. You would decide what visual aids to use. You would arrange your presentation in persuasive and streamlined form. In this way, you would apply the technique of deep analysis.

6. *Search for needs.* William J. French, Kimberly-Clark's dynamic vice-president of consumer sales, gave an assignment to his 400 salesmen. He asked each of them to answer the question: Who else needs Kleenex? A list of almost 500 new outlets and uses of Kleenex was the result. This led to another upsurge in Kleenex sales—more sales than all the sales of the more than 350 competitive brands.

Who else needs the products or services you sell? Why not build a list? Keep it growing. Ask others—fellow salesmen, customers, neighbors—for suggestions. You'll be amazed at the valuable contributions you'll get. Large companies spend huge sums on research and development—posing questions, getting answers, finding new ways to satisfy old needs, create new. You can do the same without any cash outlay.

7. *Search for improvements.* Think of the oldest style of automobile you can recall—a Model T Ford, for example. Contrast its appearance with the latest models. Why

did it take so many years to achieve the improvements? Because evolution is like that. It proceeds by slow degrees, through constant search of ways to improve this or that detail.

Life insurance salesmen years ago walked many miles every day collecting small premiums. Housewives would save 50 cents a week to pay on "burial insurance." One salesman said, "There must be an easier, less expensive way of doing business." In time he came up with the idea that resulted in Postal Life Insurance Co.—modestly priced policies sold (and premiums collected) by mail.

The professional salesman daily searches for improvements in the operation of his territory. He sends to the regional or home office suggestions for improving his company's products, packaging, services—and especially his own way of doing business.

8. *Search for defects*. This technique is closely related to the search for improvements. "What defects can I find in my present method of operation, products, services?" This excellent question is full of constructive possibilities—if followed by ways to correct the defects.

You may attribute the defects to your company's mismanagement. Your challenge then is to "sell" your suggestions to management tactfully. This means—as William M. Givens, Jr. says in his book *Reaching Out in Management*—doing something constructive about it without tramping on anybody's toes. Here you have an opportunity to practice the finest kind of creative thinking and persuasion.

9. *View ideas through the eyes of another*. The owner of a chain of toy stores gives his two children credit for his success. When he opened his first toy store, his boy was eight, his girl eleven. He took them on his buying trips— was guided by their preferences. He advertised "toys

chosen by children." He continues to consult youngsters before making his purchases. Result: His chain has grown faster than any other of its like.

When you view your products or services through the eyes of your buyers, you practice creative thinking. The whole consumer research movement has grown on this principle. As a professional salesman you'll want to make constant use of it.

10. *Make use of daydreaming.* On noticing the evening star as he was driving home, a salesman thought of a line of poetry—a favorite of his high school English teacher: "Fair as a star when only one is shining in the sky." He had recently bought some shares of Food Fair Stores, Inc. He said to himself, "Why not 'Food Fair Stars' as a slogan for week-end specials?" As he drove along, he rejected this for a substitute, "Food Fair Features," and sent it on as a suggestion.

Daydreaming—fleeting, often idealized thought—may be a source of ideas. The challenge is to follow through—to build on the vagrant idea or association.

In our daydreams we may posit, "How can I make $1,000 grow into $100,000?" If we stop with the conclusion "That would be nice!"—or begin to spend the $100,000—the daydream is nothing but a pleasant reverie. If, however, we follow through with a well-designed investment program, we may well build a fortune.

The salesman who daydreams that he's going to become vice-president in charge of marketing of a big company is thinking creatively—if he proceeds to map out a program of self-improvement to reach that high status.

11. *Collect facts on a specific subject.* Alex Osborn— famous advertising leader, author of *Your Creative Power* and many other books on how to use your imagination— was once assigned the Procter & Gamble account, one of

the largest advertisers. Osborn knew nothing about soap.
He spent hours in the New York Public Library collecting
heaps of facts about soap and human skin and hair. Result
was many highly successful advertising campaigns for Ivory
soap.

Interior decorators, dress designers, milliners collect facts
about styles from the days of the Pharaohs on down. They
convert them and sell them as the *dernier cri*.

What are the facts? (What a basic question to all the
professions!) *The Statistical Abstract of the U.S.* (published
annually in Washington by the U.S. Government Printing
Office), lists facts and statistics of many lines of activities of
interest to salesmen. For example, figures for chain stores,
mail order houses, and indexes of department store sales
are carried forward from 1959. The U.S. Bureau of the
Census supplies additional publications of interest to salesmen and sales executives, publications such as *County
Business Patterns, Census of Manufactures, Census of
Wholesaling, Census of Retailing*. It's a fact that the professional salesman can never know enough about his job.
As he accumulates reliable information and uses it to upgrade the management of his responsibilities, he adds to
his professional status.

12. *Keep a scrapbook.* If advertising at its best is printed
salesmanship, then you'll find value in filling a scrapbook
of the best advertisements. Compare and contrast your competitors' and your company's ads.

What benefits and advantages do they stress? Any good
ones omitted? How do your company's advertisements
measure up to those of the leaders in American business
and industry? Some professional salesmen keep an annual
scrapbook of the 100 best advertisements. They use them
to get ideas for their sales presentations. They study the
simplicity and pulling power of the copy. They use them

as a dynamic text on advertising. Into your scrapbook also go especially attractive sales letters, brochures, handbills, and bulletins.

13. *Keep a bushel for ideas.* Into it—or Manila folders for your files—put your gleanings—ideas picked up in conversation; tear sheets of articles that stimulated your thinking; digests of articles, chapters, or whole books; general information you may want to review; ideas for holiday promotions; curious and arresting facts.

Have you ever had this experience? An idea comes to mind which you're sure you needn't write down because you just know you'll never forget it? And then later you cudgel your brains for it? To no avail?

The experience is so common that he who depends upon ideas for his livelihood should keep a notebook in his pocket. Jot down the idea when it occurs. File it for future reference if you don't apply it right away. One suggestion more: Go through your collection occasionally. You'll find the experience interesting and rewarding. Keep those items especially that you like on second reading.

14. *Share ideas in conversation and discussion.* Salesmen ordinarily have no difficulty conversing with strangers. On an airplane or train they meet business and professional men with ideas. A salesman of eye glasses picked up the idea of bifocal lenses made from a single piece of glass from a physicist on an ocean voyage. He went into business for himself and became a millionaire.

"Share" is the word. Actually, by sharing your ideas you increase them. Somehow or other, the sharing process ensures the stream of ideas against drying up. In conversation, according to La Rochefoucauld, "Ideas often flash across our minds more complete than we could make them after much labor."

15. *Evaluate your competitors' sales promotions.* A lot

of time and expensive talent are expended on sales promotion. Ordinarily they result from the cooperative efforts of many gifted people in the sales, advertising, and merchandising departments. Sales promotions are ideas in action. Learn—from talking with customers and buyers, for example—what makes the promotions succeed. How can they be improved? What adaptations can you make of them in your sales work? What association and analogies do they bring forth?

16. *Define your terms.* Charles F. Kettering, General Motors' late great head of research, used to tell how his first famous invention—the Delco self-starter—resulted from definition. When cranking his Model T Ford one cold morning, he almost broke his arm. He said, "There must be a way to start the motor automatically." After returning home from work he jotted down six obstacles that would have to be overcome before he could start the motor automatically. He arranged the steps, from simple to complex, and began to solve them—and others as they developed—one at a time. In speaking to his research teams many years later, he always stressed the basic need to define what you want to achieve. His motto: "A problem well defined is a problem half solved!"

The need of definition in our lives recurs. Who can't profit, for instance, from a periodic definition of his job? His definition might take the form of a three-part classification: routine, unnecessary, and creative activities. Many a sales executive discovers his creativity grows in proportion to the number of "unnecessary" activities he drops or delegates to others.

17. *Schedule a daily period of concentration.* The period doesn't have to be long—ten to fifteen minutes are better than none at all. It should, however, be a regular part of your daily routine. A few can concentrate amidst noise and

confusion. Most of us must be alone and quiet to do our best thinking. "Sitting in the silence," the Quakers call it. They attribute their inspired thoughts to contemplation in deep quietude.

During the period of concentration, think hard on the problem, develop the ability—through practice—to shut out extraneous matters. "Center down"—which is what concentrate means—and succeed in getting valuable ideas.

18. *Practice brainstorming.* A group of bank executives recently met to explore the question, How can we apply marketing techniques to our bank to make it a more dynamic, a more successful, a more profitable organization? In one afternoon—using Alex Osborn's rules for conducting brainstorming sessions—they totaled 1,003 suggestions. Next day they evaluated these and selected the 411 suggestions that could be applied immediately!

Many sales training programs now include brainstorming sessions. Here amidst the stimulation of many minds the individual sparks ideas.

Here are the rules for brainstorming:

a. The group should have a leader to give the rules, recognize volunteers in order, maintain the right climate.

b. The group should not be large—five to ten is enough.

c. "Judicial judgment is ruled out." Criticism of suggestions should be avoided until all the suggestions are made.

d. Welcome "wildness." Ridicule and criticism of any suggestion are ruled out. "The crazier the idea the better.... It's easier to tone down than to think up."

e. Strive for quantity of ideas. "The more ideas pile up, the more likelihood of winners." Keep the tempo fast.

f. Encourage combinations and improvements. Say "Hitch on," when you have an idea suggested by one just given. For example, a banker said, "Let's put a drive-in window at each of our branches." Someone yelled, "Hitch on: Let's put the prettiest teller in the branch at the drive-in window."

g. Record the suggestions for future reference and study.

Batten, Barton, Durstine & Osborn attributes much of its success—it's one of the three largest advertising agencies —to brainstorming sessions. One of its sessions resulted in 45 suggestions for a home appliance client; another produced 56 ideas for a fund-raising campaign; a third developed 124 ideas on how to sell more electric blankets. At their New York office, they organized 150 of their people into 15 separate brainstorming groups on the same subject. They came forth with more than 800 ideas, 177 of which became concrete, usable suggestions.

A senior salesman in Chicago has three assistants. The four meet once a month to brainstorm a specific problem. Aside from the valuable ideas and suggestions they uncover, they report these benefits:

a. We have fun.

b. We develop teamwork.

c. We like the rivalry that facilitates the idea flow.

d. We get many more ideas—at least 400 per cent more —this way than working alone.

e. Every time one of us comes up with an idea, he automatically nudges his own imagination toward another idea.

f. At the same time, he stimulates the ideas of the other three.

Dr. Linus Carl Pauling, Caltech's famous chemist says, "The best way to have a good idea is to have lots of ideas." His theory about the nature of the chemical bond—the forces that make atoms stick together—resulted from many ideas and won for him the Nobel Prize in 1954. "Satisfaction of one's curiosity is one of the greatest sources of happiness in life," says Pauling. Professional salesmen find this so too. They satisfy their curiosity about their job by practicing such idea-provoking techniques as the 18 reviewed in this chapter. That's why, according to Anne Heywood, "We must treat ideas somewhat as though they were baby fish. Throw thousands out into the waters. Only a handful will survive, but that is plenty."

17

How to Reach and Grasp the Positive Thought

Give me the benefit of your conviction, but keep your doubts to yourself, for I have enough of my own.

GOETHE

The secret of dynamic people and organizations

Chrysler Corporation's dynamic chairman, L. L. (Tex) Colbert, ran an airplane engine plant in Chicago during World War II. When he took over the heavy responsibility, he called together his department heads. He talked to them in this vein: "If I hear anybody say that this plane won't be built on time; that the engine won't take it; that the ship won't fly; that this airplane won't win the war; that we won't be able to maintain our production schedule; that the other fellow—or his department—is the cause of your slowdown ... if I hear anything but positive, affirmative thinking expressed ... I am going to ask immediately for your resignation. Our job is to help win the war. And we're going to do just that!" Is it any wonder, under that kind of leadership, that "Tex" Colbert's plant won the highest production honors?

Sales executive William J. (Bill) Yankus holds before all his salesmen a wonderful motto: *"It can be done!"* With it, his salesmen accomplish great things. And Harry E. Whitehead, president of Toronto's Sales Executive Club recommends to his salesmen this thought: "The world is moving so fast that the man who says it can't be done is generally interrupted by someone doing it." Professor I. I. Rabi, Nobel Prize winner, explains creative thinking in atomic physics as something that requires and is worthy of basic "optimism of the possible."

The secret of all dynamic people and organizations is the positive thinking of a Tex Colbert, a Bill Yankus, a Harry Whitehead, a Professor Rabi. As a professional salesman, you wish to excel. You want to carve out a distinguished career for yourself. To do so, you'll agree, you have to reach for and hold on to constructive thinking—constantly.

In the course of your professional career you'll have your share of disappointments. You must train your attitude to take them in stride. You must keep your mind filled with wholesome, constructive plans. You must find ways and means of fostering the constructive, affirmative, positive attitude—particularly if you're given to doubts, worries, fears, or depressions.

Cultivate creative thinkers

One excellent way to promote positive thoughts is through association with those who hold the affirmative attitude. Seek out those who are optimistic, forward looking, those who stimulate ideas in you. Make friends of them. Ask their counsel. Study their way of doing things. Notice how they express themselves. Make a joint sales call occasionally with them. Study the air of plausibility they put on all things. They never doubt there's a way to be found—and they usually find it. Through your companionship with them you'll gain much that is useful in your professional and private life.

Mimic the image builder

According to the kind of presentation they make, you can classify salesmen by three main types:

1. The order taker
2. The logician
3. The image builder

Given similar territories—let them make the same number of calls—and the image builder will sell more and bigger orders—at least 100 per cent more than his runner-up, the logician.

Classification of salesmen

Here are three short presentations by salesmen—the order taker, the logician, the image builder. (Each of them is trying to persuade Mr. Brown to buy a carload of chestnut-size anthracite. Notice the sales situation is the same. The words—the image makers—make the difference.)

THE ORDER TAKER: Morning, Mr. Brown. How are Mrs. Brown and the youngsters? Been fishing lately? By the way, how's business? Got anything on the hook for me today? I surely would like to take your order for a car of chestnut.

BUYER: Sorry, Sam. Don't need any today. Drop in the next time you're in the neighborhood. So long!

THE LOGICIAN: (1) Good morning, Mr. Brown. Because I see you're very busy, I just want two minutes of your time to let me sell you a carload of chestnut. (2) Our chestnut is priced right. (3) As you know, it's tops in quality. (4) It's a better quality coal than you have been using. (5) Your customers will get a lot of satisfaction from using it. (6) You can take my word for it, or phone Frank Coal Company for confirmation. (7) I can give you many more reasons, Mr. Brown, but certainly these are convincing enough.

BUYER: Sounds reasonable, Joe, the way you put it. But there's a fly in the ointment. I don't need any right now. Maybe two or three weeks from now. So long!

THE IMAGE BUILDER: (1) Good morning, Mr. Brown. Isn't it grand, the fine comeback anthracite is making this year? (2) Colder weather and more aggressive promotion among many of our dealers have upped tonnage. (3) As you know —from reading Anthracite Institute's bulletin—we haven't been able to keep up with dealers' orders in all sizes— business is so good. Why, last month our dealers took ten per cent more tonnage than last year! (4) They like especially our chestnut—by size and burning characteristics. it's the best our company has produced in thirty years. The new-style screens we've just installed are really producing a beautiful chestnut. (5) Here is a cellophane bag of new chestnut and here is a bag of chestnut before our new screens were installed—you can see the difference. (6) It's the kind of quality product—as you can see—to keep your customers happy, reduce expensive service calls, give you higher profits in dollars—and more good will for the Brown Coal Company. (7) I have here a plan prepared for you, Mr. Brown, to move 75 tons of chestnut into your customers' bins next week—that's just one car. You see, this is just a trial order really. I predict that on my next visit you'll want to give me a real fat order—a stocking-up order.

BUYER: Sounds okay. What's your plan?

Comparison and contrast

Let's compare the logician's presentation with the image builder's (the order taker's is scarcely worthy of consideration).

Statement 1. The logician sets out rather abruptly to impose his thinking on the buyer. Most buyers resent this. The buyer may silently say, "You're not going to sell me a carload of chestnut."

The image builder deftly paints a pleasant image for the buyer—a booming business, a sellers' market.

Statement 2. The logician makes a flat, general claim about price, but price alone means little. Moreover, the buyer may disagree with the claim that it's priced *right*. Notice that the logician suggests no picture or image in the sentence. It's simply a premise that he states.

The image builder suggests two favorable (happy) business developments—colder weather, aggressive promotion —that have helped sales. If the buyer hasn't shared in the expanding market, he begins to wonder why. And his curiosity is aroused.

Statement 3. The logician here again gives a plain, unvarnished statement about the quality of his company's chestnut.

The image builder jam-packs his statement with the dynamic suggestions of "good business," "10 per cent more tonnage than last year," "production behind demand," and backs them up with authority (Anthracite Institute's bulletin). If the buyer were to admit that his own business isn't like that, he would lose face. If he admitted it, he would give the salesman an opportunity to show him how to bring his business up to par. The point is, in either event the salesman keeps the point of vantage.

Statement 4. The logician tries again to dominate the buyer by a flat statement that makes him feel inferior. By depreciating the buyer's judgment—in buying competitive coal—the salesman actually arouses feelings of antagonism and ill will (even though the salesman's statement may be entirely true).

The image builder identifies the top quality of his product with *successful* coal dealers—and accounts for its superior quality by mentioning four advantages: (*a*) larger size, (*b*) better burning characteristics, (*c*) "best in thirty years," and (*d*) the new-style screens. Here again we have constructive, specific appeals to the mind of the buyer—all of which add up to a pleasant, reassuring picture.

Statement 5. The logician once more makes a flat, colorless, hackneyed, unimaginative statement: "Your customers will get a lot of satisfaction from using it."

The image builder presents the buyer with a visual aid, two bags of chestnut, "before" and "after" the new-style screens were installed. But notice: The salesman had already prepared the mind of the buyer to see the excellence of the new product—now put before him—to contrast it by sight and touch with the old.

Statement 6. The logician, when he says, "You can take my word for it . . ." actually plants seeds of doubt in the buyer's mind. He's teaching him sin.

The image builder proceeds to pique the buyer's desire by dangling before his eyes vistas of happy customers, fewer (expensive) service calls, more profits, more prestige for the company.

Statement 7. The logician ends weakly, saying he could offer more reasons. He implies that he's worked hard enough, that Mr. Brown—unless he's stupid—ought to be convinced by now. Moreover, the logician doesn't actually propose an order or a course of action. He opens the door wide for a turndown.

The image builder closes strong—with a specific suggestion, with a plan to help. He continues to paint an image of helpfulness—an adventure in togetherness. And the buyer goes along as a matter of course. The image builder has led the buyer's mind into green pastures.

Assignment

1. Review your most recent sales presentation. Which of them resembled the image builder's? the logician's? the order taker's?

2. Write a sales presentation dealing with your own product or service in which you use the logician's approach.

3. Write another sales presentation in which you use the image builder's approach. Make it longer, if necessary, than the example.

4. Share your two presentations with a fellow salesman or sales executive. Discuss them in detail.

5. Deliver your image-builder presentation aloud. Have one of your fellow salesmen or sales executives play the role of the buyer.

6. Carry over into your daily work the suggestion of creating happy images in the mind of the buyer.

Follow these suggestions daily. You'll train yourself to choose your words—and present your thoughts—to arouse pleasing, cheerful, positive ideas and associations. Develop this precious skill and you'll sell rings around the order takers or cold logicians.

Keep in mind the advice of C. W. Dilley, president of the Lehigh Navigation Coal Company, to his salesmen: "Our responsibility as creative salesmen goes beyond being cheerful in the presence of the customer. We must create in his mind thoughts and feelings of success, profit, efficiency, growth!"

Your impact on others

Your success depends upon the effect of your outgoing personality and constructive ideas—on your fellow salesmen, subordinates, executives, and customers.

As a salesman you have a double value to your company.

First is the value measured by your job performance: how you manage your territory, growth of your sales, quality of your promotions, your customer relations, how you cooperate with your executives and the office, how well you play the role of teammate, etc.

Second is the value reflected by your influence on others. Let's call it the 1-0-0 Factor. This value is very real, just as real and valuable as your job performance—often more so.

Fact is, your over-all job performance can't possibly be first rate unless your 1-0-0 Factor is high. When your 1-0-0 Factor excels, management rewards you with increases, often with promotions to greater responsibility.

Study the great salesmen—the most successful sales executives. Both groups distinguish themselves by the wholesome, constructive, inspiring influence they exert on others at three levels: those of equal rank, those who work for them, those for whom they work.

As you work to build your career, the 1-0-0 Factor means more and more—to you and to those who manage your company. For this reason, you'll want to study the appraisal profile below. With it you can measure your 1-0-0 Factor. All you have to do is:

1. Circle the percentage you believe represents your present development. In this way, you rate yourself.

2. Get someone close to you to rate you. This will help you to check on your judgment of self.

3. Discuss the results with your wife, supervisor, division manager, or fellow salesman. By being open-minded you'll find it an interesting and valuable experience.

Here are the 10 ways to rate your influence on others:

1. *Courtesy*   100   75   50   **25**
    (freedom from undue familiarity, sarcasm, boisterousness; habits
    of polite practices)
2. *Empathy*   100   75   50   25

(ability to feel yourself into the state of mind and predicament
of others and respond accordingly)

3. *Kindness*   100   75   50   25
(doing thoughtful deeds and speaking helpful words to others
without being or seeming condescending)

4. *Manners*   100   75   50   25
(personal conduct at table, in acknowledging introductions, helping to carry conversations, and other deportment in social con-
gress)

5. *Humility*   100   75   50   25
(attitude of being deferential to the other fellow and his point
of view, reluctance to impose egotism in situations of group
thinking, practice of trying to learn from everyone)

6. *Expectance*   100   75   50   25
(attitude of believing that people are potentially greater than
they think they are; holding great expectations of others; assuming wholesome motivations on the part of others unless incon-
testable *proof* is forthcoming to the contrary)

7. *Constructiveness*   100   75   50   25
(by thought, word, vocal inflection, facial expression, bearing
and action making company policy a way of life, an attitude
that encourages others to look to you for leadership and the
forward march)

8. *Cultural responsibility*   100   75   50   25
(through reading, study, and family life representing the best
that has been thought and said)

9. *Growth*   100   75   50   25
(demonstrating through the constant upgrading of personal
habits and attitudes that you believe in "the one increasing
purpose," that thereby job satisfaction increases, and that there
is no pleasure to take the place of achievement in helping to build
a more dynamic, profitable company)

10. *Spirituality*   100   75   50   25
(the belief that divine expression is in every man as well as in
nature, that prayer is important in daily life, that the chief end
of life is to develop insight to understand "the ways of God to
man")

Now that you have rated yourself—and obtained a
check-up rating from a friend—what specifically do you
plan to do to increase your total score?

Look for the positive approach in case studies.

Case studies provide you with descriptions of sales successes and failures. When you study them you extend your selling experience enormously. You make use of the trial and error—trial and success—of other salesmen. You pick up ideas of what and what not to do—without actually going through the motions. You simply beckon to experienced salesmen, and they come running—to teach you free of charge.

Case studies

Where to find case studies on salesmanship? In many places: (1) textbooks, such as *Case Problems in Creative Salesmanship* by K. B. Haas (Prentice-Hall, Inc., Englewood Cliffs, N.J.); (2) occasional pieces in *Sales Management, Fortune, Forbes, Business Week, Advertising & Selling,* etc.; (3) salesmen's biographies and autobiographies, such as Frank Bettger's, *How I Raised Myself from Failure to Success in Selling* (Prentice-Hall, Inc., Englewood Cliffs, N.J.); (4) case studies provided by the Harvard University School of Business Administration, American Management Association, etc.

Let's consider a case study of a most successful salesman. After you read it, you can answer some questions about it. As you supply the answers, you'll develop a technique for analyzing case studies in salesmanship. You can then apply your findings to your own ways of selling to increase the positive, the winning approach.

Case of the high-pressure salesman

This case study is told by the late great Wall Street operator Livingston in Edwin Lefevre's *Reminiscences of a Stock Operator* (The Sun Dial Press, Inc., New York, 1938).

One day just after the market closed I heard somebody say, "Good afternoon, Mr. Livingston."

I turned and saw an utter stranger—a chap of about thirty or thirty-five. I could not understand how he'd got in, but there he was. I concluded, his business with me had passed him. But I didn't say anything. I just looked at him and pretty soon he said, "I came to see you about that Walter Scott," and he was off.

He was a book salesman. Now, he was not especially attractive to look at. But he certainly had personality. He talked and I thought I listened. But I do not know what he said. I don't think I ever knew, not even at the time. When he finished his monologue he handed me first his fountain pen and then a blank form, which I signed. It was a contract to take a set of Scott's works for five hundred dollars.

The moment I signed I came to. But he had the contract safe in his pocket. I did not want the books. I had no place for them. They weren't of any use whatever to me. I had nobody to give them to. Yet I had agreed to buy them for five hundred dollars.

I am so accustomed to losing money that I never think first of that phase of my mistakes. It is always the play itself, the reason why. In the first place I wish to know my own limitations and habits of thought. Another reason is that I do not wish to make the same mistake a second time. A man can excuse his mistakes only by capitalizing them to his subsequent profit.

Well, having made a five-hundred dollar mistake but not yet having localized the trouble, I just looked at the fellow to size him up as a first step. I'll be hanged if he didn't actually smile at me—an understanding little smile! He seemed to read my thoughts. I somehow knew that I did not have to explain anything to him; he knew it without my telling him. So I skipped the explanations and the preliminaries and asked him, "How much commission will you get on that five hundred dollar order?"

He promptly shook his head and said, "I can't do it! Sorry!"

"How much do you get?" I persisted.

"A third. But I can't do it!" he said.

"A third of five hundred dollars is one hundred and sixty-six dollars and sixty-six cents. I'll give you two hundred dollars cash if you give me back that signed contract." And to prove it I took the money out of my pocket.

"I told you I couldn't do it," he said.

"Do all your customers make the same offer to you?" I asked.

"No," he answered.

"Then why were you so sure that I was going to make it?"

"It is what your type of sport would do. You are a first-class loser and that makes you a first-class businessman. I am much obliged to you, but I can't do it."

"Now tell me why you do not wish to make more than your commission?"

"It isn't that, exactly," he said. "I am not working just for commission."

"What are you working for then?"

"For the commission and the record," he answered.

"What record?"

"Mine."

"What are you driving at?"

"Do you work for money alone?" he asked me.

"Yes," I said.

"No." And he shook his head. "No, you don't. You wouldn't get enough fun out of it. You certainly do not work merely to add a few more dollars to your bank account, and you are not in Wall Street because you like easy money. You get your fun some other way. Well, same here."

I did not argue but asked him, "And how do you get your fun?"

"Well," he confessed, "we've all got a weak spot."

"And what's yours?"

"Vanity," he said.

"Well," I told him, "you succeeded in getting me to sign on. Now I want to sign off, and I am paying you two hundred dollars for ten minutes' work. Isn't that enough for your pride?"

"No," he answered. "You see, all the rest of the bunch have been working Wall Street for months and failed to make expenses. They said it was the fault of the goods and the territory. So the office sent for me to prove that the fault was with their salesmanship and not with the books or the place. They were working on a 25 per cent commission. I was in Cleveland, where I sold eighty-two sets in two weeks. I am here to sell a certain number of sets not only to people who did not buy from the other agents but to people they couldn't even get to see. That's why they give me $33\frac{1}{3}$ per cent."

"I can't quite figure out how you sold me that set."

"Why," he said consolingly, "I sold J. P. Morgan a set."

"No, you didn't," I said.

He wasn't angry. He simply said, "Honest, I did!"

"A set of Walter Scott to J. P. Morgan, who not only has some fine editions but probably the original manuscript of some of the novels as well?"

"Well, here's his John Hancock." And he promptly flashed on me a contract signed by J. P. Morgan himself. It might not have been Mr. Morgan's signature, but it did not occur to me to doubt it at the time. Didn't he have mine in his pocket? All I felt was curiosity. So I asked him, "How did you get past the librarian?"

"I didn't see any librarian. I saw the Old Man himself in his office."

"That's too much!" I said. Everybody knew that it was much harder to get into Mr. Morgan's private office empty handed than into the White House with a parcel that ticked like an alarm clock.

But he declared, "I did."

"But how did you get into his office?"

"How did I get into yours?" he retorted.

"I don't know. You tell me," I said.

"Well, the way I got into Morgan's office and the way I got

into yours are the same. I just talked to the fellow at the door whose business it was not to let me in. And the way I got Morgan to sign was the same way I got you to sign. You weren't signing a contract for a set of books. You just took the fountain pen I gave you and did what I asked you to do with it. No difference. Same as you."

"And is that really Morgan's signature?" I asked him, about three minutes late with my skepticism.

"Sure! He learned how to write his name when he was a boy."

"And that's all there's to it?"

"That's all," he answered. "I know exactly what I am doing. That's all the secret there is. I am much obliged to you. Good day, Mr. Livingston." And he started to go out.

"Hold on," I said. "I'm bound to have you make an even two hundred dollars out of me." And I handed him thirty-five dollars.

He shook his head. Then: "No," he said. "I can't do that. But I can do this!" And he took the contract from his pocket, tore it in two and gave me the pieces.

I counted two hundred dollars and held the money before him, but he again shook his head.

"Isn't that what you meant?" I said.

"No."

"Then why did you tear up the contract?"

"Because you did not whine, but took it as I would have taken it myself had I been in your place."

"But I offered you the two hundred dollars of my own accord," I said.

"I know; but money isn't everything."

Something in his voice made me say, "You're right; it isn't. And now what do you really want me to do for you?"

"You're quick, aren't you?" he said. "Do you really want to do something for me?"

"Yes," I told him, "I do. But whether I will or not depends on what it is you have in mind."

"Take me with you into Mr. Ed Harding's office and tell

him to let me talk to him three minutes by the clock. Then, leave me alone with him."

I shook my head and said, "He is a good friend of mine," "He's fifty years old and a stock broker," said the book agent.

That was perfectly true, so I took him into Ed's office. I did not hear anything more from or about that book agent. But one evening some weeks later when I was going uptown I ran across him in a Sixth Avenue L train. He raised his hat very politely and I nodded back. He came over and asked me, "How do you do, Mr. Livingston? And how is Mr. Harding?"

"He's well. Why do you ask?" I felt he was holding back a story.

"I sold him two thousand dollars' worth of books that day you took me in to see him."

"He never said a word to me about it," I said.

"No; that kind doesn't talk about it."

"What kind doesn't talk?"

"The kind that never makes mistakes on account of its being bad business to make them. That kind always knows what he wants and nobody can tell him different. That is the kind that's educating my children and keeps my wife in good humor. You did me a good turn, Mr. Livingston. I expected it when I gave up the two hundred dollars you were so anxious to present to me."

"And if Mr. Harding hadn't given you an order?"

"Oh, but I knew he would. I had found out what kind of man he was. He was a cinch."

"Yes. But if he hadn't bought any books?" I persisted.

"I'd have come back to you and sold you something. Good day, Mr. Livingston. I am going to see the mayor." And he got up as we pulled up at Park Place.

"I hope you sell him ten sets," I said. His Honor was a Tammany man.

"I'm a Republican too," he said, and went out, not hastily, but leisurely, confident that the train would wait. And it did.

Assignment

Here are 10 questions to help you analyze case studies. Answer them in detail.

1. What attitudes did the book salesman reveal? Which were helpful to him in the selling situation? Which did you admire? Which did you not admire?

2. How do your own attitudes compare with the book salesman's?

3. As a professional salesman, how would you estimate the ethics of the sale?

4. How did the book salesman gain and hold the attention of his buyer?

5. Did he mention any benefits or advantages—reasons for buying?

6. How do you visualize the salesman? What were the main traits of his personality?

7. Do you believe his sales presentation was "canned"; or did he "play it by ear"? Why?

8. Can you offer suggestions on how he might have improved the presentation?

9. What would you do differently in similar circumstances?

10. How many specific suggestions did you get from the case study—suggestions you can use to improve your own sales performance?

18

How to Profit from and Enjoy Sales Meetings

> Whenever two or more successful salesmen sit down together you're bound to have a sales meeting.
>
> E. J. THOMAS

Millions for meetings

A hundred and fifty million dollars is a lot of money. That's an estimate of the annual cost of sales meetings in the United States and Canada. Sales meetings are therefore a big investment in our enterprise system—a spark plug of our dynamic economy. They must pay off, else management wouldn't invest increasing sums in them.

Kinds of meetings

Sales meetings range from small periodic training groups to large annual conclaves. They include conventions, brainstorming sessions, divisional and regional get-togethers, professional seminars. They may last an hour or spread over

236

several weeks. Ordinarily they have four purposes in common: to give information, to receive information, to improve sales performance, to build morale. Although he may
find some meetings—or parts of meetings—more rewarding than others, the professional salesman can make each
one he attends more efficient, more profitable, more stimulating, more enjoyable—and he has a responsibility to do so.

How can he help?

Here are a few suggestions.

1. *Look for personal benefits and advantages throughout the entire meeting.* Always remember there's no such
thing as an uninteresting subject; there are only uninter-
ested people.

A salesman recently complained he's bored with some
parts of his company's annual sales meeting. He singles out
the treasurer, who customarily reads price lists. These
could be distributed instead and thus save time. (Eventually they are distributed.) But the treasurer is an officer,
and the sales manager finds it tactful to have the treasurer
on the program. Because he's a wretched public speaker, he
reads.

Now the point is the salesman fails to take advantage of
the treasurer's part in the program. Instead of grousing or
taking a nap—with or without the eyes closed—the salesman can review, for example, the techniques of reading
aloud.

Reading aloud questionnaire

  a. Does the treasurer survey his audience to gain atten-
     tion before he begins?
  b. How gracious and competent are his salutation and
     opening remarks?
  c. Does he read communicatively—glancing up fre-

quently at various parts of the audience as he reads from his manuscript?

d. How are his posture and breath control?

e. Which words does he mispronounce? Which sounds does he slur or mangle?

f. What about the intonations of his voice—pleasant or monotonous?

g. Does he shift gears as he reads? Does he read fast, slow, and medium from time to time to give variety?

h. Does he use facial expressions, gestures, and postures to enrich his spoken communication?

i. Does he group his words and pause so as to help his hearers grasp the thoughts of the sentences easily?

j. Does he read loud enough and project his voice adequately?

k. If he uses a microphone, does he use it well?

l. Does he have any mannerisms that detract?

Why, the salesman using the treasurer as a guinea pig can give himself a refresher course in the right and wrong way to read aloud! And doing so, he's so constructively busy there isn't a second for boredom! Everybody wins!

Thus, all's grist for the professional salesman's mill. He can turn every minute and experience at a sales meeting to his advantage because he's open-minded and eager to learn.

2. *Encourage speakers to do their best.* The French expression for "to attend a meeting" is *assister.* The implication is that you help even if you're not on the program. Now, this is an excellent concept. To get the most from a program, be attentive. Look at the speaker, assist him by listening to him actively. Let him see encouragement and respect for his point of view in your face and posture.

If there's a question-and-answer period, help the speaker by putting an intelligent question succinctly. Think it through. Perhaps you'll want to write it first and revise it, if necessary, before you ask it. When he recognizes you, address him by name before you ask the question. Of course you'll ask questions—or make suggestions—tactfully. Don't imply criticisms in them. You won't monopolize the floor, or be mute if you have something of value to say. You'll speak up—loud and clear so that everyone can hear you with ease.

3. *Come prepared.* Because sales meetings cost so much, each year more effort goes into planning them. (By the way, do you read *Sales Meetings,* published six times a year by Bill Brothers Publications Co., 630 Third Avenue, New York City?) Often instructions go out to salesmen before the meeting—about transportation, housing, dress, expenses, etc. Sometimes you receive the program a week or two in advance to help you prepare for the meeting.

Suppose you've received the program for your next annual sales meeting. It's organized around "Meet the Men behind You." You notice that each major department head of your company will speak. You notice also there's going to be a question-and-answer period at the end of each presentation.

To prepare for this program you may want to review your company's organization chart, your sales instruction manual, and your company's latest annual report to the stockholders. Why not jot down questions as they occur to you before you attend the meeting? You may be especially interested in departmental policies and procedures.

For example, you may want to ask the vice-president in charge of finance about the company's stock option plan. Or, you may have a special interest in the advertising manager's attitude toward consumer research. If the head of research and development speaks, you may have a question for him about new products.

Some of your questions, the speakers may anticipate. Others won't be covered. Anyway you'll be prepared. Thus both your interest in the meeting and your capacity to profit from it increases.

4. *Take notes.* Try to see how many ideas you can jot down. Later on, as you study them, the meeting will continue to pay you dividends long after it's over. Date your notes by half days (see Chapter 14).

5. *Lend a helping hand.* Perhaps you can help a friend with the props he's going to use in his presentation. If somebody forgets to open a window, undertake the responsibility. Perhaps you can volunteer to help distribute material. Maybe a colleague of yours would like you to listen to him rehearse his presentation. You may write well on a blackboard and be a speaker's blackboard secretary. Doing such deeds modestly helps the efficiency and morale of meetings.

6. *Make the most of contacts.* The Young Presidents Organization is remarkable. As you probably know, to be a member you must be under forty and the head of a business employing at least 10, doing a minimum annual gross of $1 million. More than a thousand men and women are members of YPO in the United States and Canada, and the majority of them began as salesmen. When surveyed recently about what they attribute their early success to, they mentioned contacts high on the list.

Every meeting the professional salesman attends is a field day for making contacts, for building worthy friendships. Whether at his own company meetings or elsewhere, he meets and chats with old friends and makes new ones. Bull sessions, coffee breaks, card games and the golf course, trips through the factory, companionship at the luncheon or dinner table—all offer opportunities to make contacts. Throughout these pleasant experiences always remember you're being appraised and studied. What you say and do attracts, repels, or creates apathy. The worthiest contacts are likely to be made with those who put a high value on admirable traits of personality and character. "Gossip," said David Starr Jordan, "is the first art of neighborliness." He meant, of course, the genial small talk about people, places, and things, topics for easy conversation, not backbiting or unworthy comments.

Many of the contacts you make you'll want to cultivate after the meeting ends. Perhaps you'll want to write a friendly note as a follow-up, or send a Christmas card, or exchange an idea by mail or telephone once in a while.

Many successful salesmen at company meetings single out members of other departments and make friends of them. They may cultivate the credit manager, the mail clerk or the head of the shipping or billing department. They're the men behind the firing line whose cooperation helps you to do a professional selling job.

7. *Don't overindulge.* Sales meetings are famous for calories and the red-carpet treatment. One must guard against overeating, too much drinking and smoking, particularly if the meeting is a long one. Eating, drinking, smoking sensibly, getting enough sleep and some exercise are important directives to follow to profit from prolonged meetings.

8. *Avoid the "six mistakes of man."* Sales meetings are excellent places to avoid six famous human foibles. Cicero, before the birth of Christ, spelled them out. Here they are:

a. The delusion that individual advancement is made by crushing others
b. The tendency to worry about things that cannot be changed or corrected
c. Insisting a thing is impossible because we ourselves cannot accomplish it

d. Refusing to set aside trivial preferences

e. Neglecting development and refinement of the mind, and not acquiring habits of reading and studying

f. Attempting to compel other people to believe and live as we do

How often in the affairs of a meeting does a salesman observe the six mistakes! And how much he gives to its success when he avoids and helps others to avoid them!

9. *Use your influence to upgrade the quality and value of training meetings.* A psychologist recently looked through the sales training manual of a large building supply concern. The personnel director beamed with expectancy of high praise from the psychologist. The psychologist, a rather blunt fellow, said, "I don't see any evidence of sales training in your manual. What you have, it seems to me, is an excellent collection of product information!"

Many so-called sales training meetings are simply get-togethers to discuss product information. The assumption is that the salesmen know all there's to know about selling. The point of view is that they don't need basic training in selling techniques, nor do they need to review them.

And right here is where management is so wrong. For just as the surgeon has to practice techniques—and under supervision—so the professional salesman needs refresher courses. He's like the opera singer with good voice and knowledge of arias who must continue to coach long after he's achieved distinction.

Let's therefore conclude this chapter by discussing only one valuable technique to use in sales training meetings. It's worth so much that some successful companies use it at least once each year with all their salesmen. It never becomes boring through reuse because it provides so much that's ever new and always profitable. We call it the "activated case study" (ACS). It includes exercise in account analysis, writing, public speaking, role playing, making visual aids, conducting a conference, brainstorming, blackboard technique, evaluation, follow-up. Let's describe it in some detail.

Ways to benefit from ACS

1. *Arrangements.* Let's assume you're a member of a sales training group—20 or fewer salesmen. If the meeting covers several days, all of you can each present an ACS of your own. If your group has only a half day to devote to it, you can participate even if you don't present one.

Ideally the group should be seated behind continuous tables, arranged in a horseshoe. At the open end you should have a low dais, large enough for a table and two chairs. At the side, on the floor, have a blackboard on casters.

You'll probably receive a notice of the meeting and arrangements and also an assignment.

2. *The assignment.* Write an actual case study based on a sales problem you have with one of your accounts or prospects. Use the Flesch formula (see Chapter 15).

  a. Describe the prospect or account type, why selected.
  b. Describe the buyer—the kind of person he is.
  c. State your sales problem. What do you want to sell him?
  d. Describe your objective—what steps you propose to take to sell the prospect or account.

Here's an example, names disguised:

Case Study
of
XYZ Stores—South City, La.
by
JONATHAN JONES

Description of account: XYZ Stores is a chain of 32 Class A supermarkets in the South City, Louisiana, area. Two years ago they closed their small, obsolete stores. Since then they opened six new supermarkets. Next year they will open 12 more new supermarkets—one a month. They recently announced their intention to buy a small local chain of supermarkets. The company, you see, is growing. At present it ranks third in volume in my territory. Because of its aggressive management it may shortly become my most important account.

Description of buyers: Joe Black, the grocery buyer, is a stern businessman, hard to reach. His assistant, Jack White, is open-minded. But his hands are tied by Black. I know the other two men on the merchandise committee only slightly. They are buyers in other departments. All of them are afraid of the president who's active and dictatorial. He finds it hard to delegate authority.

Description of problem: XYZ Stores buy our products in less than carload orders. They buy from two of our competitors in carload orders; from a third, less than carload lots. XYZ doesn't give my competitors or me promotional support. Recently, XYZ began buying an off-brand competitive line with display and advertising support. XYZ turned down my recommendation of last August's "Volume Incentive Promotion." Now they've just turned me down on our recent VIP promotion.

Description of objective: My objective is to show XYZ buyers that our line of products is the best to fit their needs. I plan to make a presentation in which I show that our line:

  a. Has the best national and local advertising support
  b. Has the fastest turnover in stores that cooperate with us
  c. Is *the* quality line
  d. Can make more money for XYZ than any of our competitors

Now let's assume that you're asked to present your case study. Here are the other steps you follow.

3. *Read the case study to the group at the open end of the horseshoe.* (Read it as the treasurer should have read, aloud.) Give supplementary details, particularly in response to questions from the group. Your aim is to help the group understand clearly the background of your problem.

4. *Make the sales presentation on the dais.* Ask a fellow salesman or your supervisor to play the role of the buyer you plan to make your presentation to. Coach him in advance of your presentation to play the role of the buyer just as the buyer acts and speaks. You'll play the role of yourself in the selling situation. Begin with the greeting and opener just as you plan to do when you call on the XYZ company and proceed through the close.

5. *Use a visual aid.* Preferably you should have one you've prepared especially for XYZ showing your products.

6. *Ask the group to rate your presentation.* You may wish to provide them with copies of this form to do the job:

Appraisal Form for Activated Case Study Presentations

Salesman's name: _____ Date: _____

Division: _____ Place: _____

	(10)	(9)	(8)	(7)	(6)
	Excellent	*Good*	*Average*	*Poor*	*Unsatisfactory*
1. *Sales impression:* appearance, approach, clean, neat, well-groomed, alert, poised, at ease, pleasant					
2. *Selling attitude:* enthusiastic, convincing, mature, sincere					
3. *Speech:* vocabulary, voice, grammar, pronunciation					
4. *Organization of presentation:* Introduction, development, conclusion, specific answers, communication without wordiness					

Appraisal Form for Activated Case Study Presentations (cont.)

	(10) Excellent	(9) Good	(8) Average	(7) Poor	(6) Unsatis-factory
5. *Psychology:* attention, interest, desire, humor, etc.					
6. *Knowledge of subject:* facts, information					
7. *Control of interview:* effective prospect participation in the interview, adherence to objective, sharing of talking and listening					
8. *Emphasis:* reasons to buy, benefits, advantages					
9. *Objections:* recognized, handled tactfully, converted into reasons for buying					
10. *Use of sales aids:* quality and use of visual aids, use of products					
11. *Progress:* good reason for call? Was it a quality presentation? Did he leave with a planned program based on the situation? Did he ask for the order?					

7. *Conduct a discussion.* At the end of your presentation, have a discussion on "How can I improve my presentation to XYZ?" Put the blackboard in front of the dais. Ask the man who plays the role of the buyer to write the suggestions on the board as you draw them from the group seated at the tables.

8. *Use this salesman's discussion leadership questionnaire.* This will serve as a guide in helping you conduct an excellent discussion.

   a. Did the leader appraise the audience before beginning to speak?

   b. Did the leader begin with creating a friendly climate with his audience?

   c. Did the leader adequately introduce the topic for discussion?

   d. Did the leader specify the goals of the discussion?

   e. Did the leader interpret the points made by individuals to their satisfaction?

   f. Did the leader list the suggestions on the blackboard in consistent style?

   g. Did the leader play the role of servant to the group?

   h. Did the leader observe the amenities, such as calling contributors by name, calling on them in order of their volunteering, thanking them, etc.?

   i. Did the leader get coverage of all parts of the discussion group?

   j. Did the leader encourage the "reluctant dragons" to make contributions?

   k. Did the leader make use of his training in public speaking, particularly in regard to effective voice and diction, gestures and facial expression, posture and stance, etc.?

   l. Did the leader observe the time limits placed upon the discussion?

   m. Did the leader summarize the discussion in his concluding remarks?

   n. Did the leader succeed in leaving the group with the sense that the discussion was positive and helpful?

9. *Follow through.* Soon as you return to the field, make the presentation to the XYZ Company. (Of course you'll

improve your original presentation by adapting the helpful suggestions from the discussion.) Report the results to your supervisor or manager. (One company reports that three out of every four ACS's result in selling the accounts!)

10. *Take notes on all the case studies presented.* You'll be able to use the suggestions made in the discussions in your other sales presentations.

Now let's review the values of the ACS as a training technique for meetings.

1. It helps you analyze an account you want to sell by following a plan.

2. It gives you an exercise in writing.

3. It provides you with an exercise in reading aloud and public speaking—before the most difficult of audiences, your own colleagues.

4. It gives you the experience of coaching another in role playing.

5. It provides you with an opportunity to deliver a sales presentation under supervision.

6. It gives you exercise in preparing and using a tailor-made visual aid.

7. It provides you with the opportunity to lead a discussion.

8. It helps you to get ideas and suggestions from your peers on sales techniques.

9. It provides you with the benefit of getting reactions as to how you sound and appear to others.

10. It provides you with an opportunity to take notes.

11. It helps you to sell well—in the spirit and ways of professional salesmanship.

If you haven't tried the activated case study, you'll find it one of the best items for a sales meeting.

19

What Next?

> Our todays and yesterdays are the blocks
> with which we build.
>
> LONGFELLOW

Next step

In the natural course of events, you—as a professional
salesman—can expect advancement. Like the majority of
salesmen, you perhaps want to become a marketing executive. If so, your first promotion will probably be to the position of sales supervisor.

What is a sales supervisor?

Perhaps we should define our terms. A sales supervisor
is a representative of middle management. His is not an
office job, however. His work is in the field. His chief duties
are (1) to train young salesmen; (2) to upgrade older salesmen; (3) to make use with them of performance reviews and
appraisals; (4) to help his salesmen analyze their markets
and customers; (5) to interpret company policy to his men
and relay their thinking to his superiors; (6) to hold sales

and training meetings with his salesmen to exchange experiences and develop *esprit de corps;* (7) to visit his salesmen's homes occasionally to discuss the company—and the men's responsibilities to it—with their families. Other duties may be and usually are added, but these seven are basic.

In one company, the supervisor may be known as a district sales manager, in another, field sales manager. But in more successful companies there's a growing tendency to have one man in sales supervision directly responsible for the development and welfare of from 6 to 10 salesmen. He usually lives in the geographic center of the territories the salesmen travel. His responsibilities are so heavy that he cannot devote the major part of his time to desk work. Therefore, in marketing-minded, successful companies, the sales supervisor has a teammate—who is sometimes his boss—a regional or division manager. This teammate is the administrator, the office man.

Ordinarily, the sales supervisor spends five days a week in the field. He makes joint calls with his salesmen, listens to their challenges and woes; advises them, teaches them greater skill in closing sales, in providing their customers with ideas and service. Some of his on-the-job quandaries and challenges are listed at the end of this chapter.

If he is a good sales supervisor, he usually does his own paper work at night or on Saturday morning. He never uses paper work as an escape or as an excuse to dodge his primary responsibility—working with his salesmen.

Why sales supervisors?

Lewis E. Phenner, senior vice-president of marketing, Kimberly-Clark Corporation—one of the few paper companies reporting increased sales during the letdowns following World War II—attributes the success of his sales force to a number of things. At the head of the list he puts intelligent and trained sales supervision. Other leading marketing executives agree.

This conclusion confirms studies by Peter Drucker and others indicating that the chief characteristic of the dynamic American economy is heavy investment in supervision. A hundred years ago in the United States—according to estimates—for every $100 paid for wages and salaries, $5 was paid for supervision. Today for every $100 paid for salaries and wages, an estimated $30 is paid for supervision. The future will call for increased outlays for supervision. No other country approaches our outlay for supervision in the factory and office. Western Germany—the runner-up in industrial efficiency—is perhaps second today in investment in supervision, with England probably third. Note: These cost totals and averages for supervision are for factory and office work.

The United States and Canada lead in outlays for sales supervision. But the commitment is lower on a proportionate basis than in factory and office supervision. Moreover, the skills of the sales supervisor are less standardized and many believe, less efficient, than those of the factory or office supervisor.

However, if you study leading companies, such as IBM, GE, Kimberly-Clark, Canadian Pacific Railway, you'll find something significant about their investment in sales supervisors: it exceeds that of their weaker competitors proportionately. Moreover, their supervisors are better trained.

What companies do when they hire and train supervisors—whether for the factory, office, or sales division—is to provide a constant source of productive stimulation to less gifted or less experienced people.

You see, therefore, what a high honor and heavy responsibility it is to be appointed a sales supervisor. To prepare for the promotion and to succeed in it you may want to review the basic principles—of selecting, training, and developing sales supervisors.

First principle: Be a good teacher.

Your sales supervisor, as defined, is basically a teacher. Think back to teachers you had. The good ones made ideas interesting. Ordinarily they had a lot of patience. They were admirable and you tended to make heroes (or heroines) of them. They ran a good shop. You couldn't get by—they had standards you respected, and they enforced their standards firmly but fairly. They gave directions and assignments you could grasp readily. They were enthusiastic about the subject they taught. And they favored concepts more than precepts.

They seized every opportunity to apply the principle or idea discussed to parallel fields of learning and to everyday life. They could see the subject through your eyes, were sensitive to your quandaries and frustrations. They respected you as an individual and held great expectations for you. They liked people a lot and gave you the impression of wanting to be liked. They seemed to have time, or make time, for you, especially if you needed extra help. They were devoted to you and your fellow students, to ideas, and to the school. Beyond all else, they were kind. The sales supervisor cannot succeed as he should without having the qualifications of the teacher.

Very often a company selects the "best" salesman to be a sales supervisor. And this may be a grave mistake. The successful salesman is sometimes not interested in teaching. He may be too impatient with those who don't learn fast. He may take too much for granted. The great salesman may be so interested in his work he doesn't really want to instruct. He therefore is a poor or mediocre teacher.

Of course, all this doesn't mean that the competent sales supervisor should not be a good salesman. He should be a highly competent salesman with an outstanding record as a producer. But he must have the qualities of a good teacher added. And these qualities will assume greater importance in the future. So be sure you like teaching and you will make a good teacher.

Second principle: Make sure you want the job.

Ordinarily, the sales supervisor—as representative of middle management—has more prestige, by reason of his title, than the salesmen he supervises. Moreover, the sales supervisor usually makes more money than the salesman. And so, many a candidate finds it hard to refuse the offer.

However, not every candidate wants to be a sales supervisor. What are some of the common blocks to his really wanting the promotion? Let's list those observed most often.

1. *Too much travel.* A star salesman in a metropolitan market—home every night—often doesn't want to travel throughout the week as a supervisor.

2. *Moving.* The new sales supervisor sometimes has to move to a different part of the country or to another location within his district or division. He and his family may have the home they want. They may lose money, exchanging their home for a new one. (Some companies have no policy of protecting the man's losses.) The children may not want to change schools and leave their friends, etc.

3. *Fear of the unknown.* If the job is new, the candidate may not want to accept the challenge of helping to define it. He may doubt his ability to teach and lead salesmen. You meet this attitude most often in companies that have no job descriptions or training programs for sales supervisors.

4. *The wife.* If she isn't persuaded that her husband—and family—will profit from the promotion, she may influence him to reject the offer. If she's forced into the move, without being persuaded of the benefits, she may be a constant source of irritation. Under such circumstances her husband is likely to fail.

5. *Not enough pay.* Some companies don't pay their sales supervisors enough for their added responsibilities. Suppose a company selects its supervisors from among its senior salesmen. Suppose the senior salesmen have company cars while the sales supervisors don't. If the sales supervisors receive $1,000 more a year than they earned as senior salesmen, the increment isn't large enough to compensate for the loss of the company car and the assumption of added responsibility.

6. *Lack of confidence in management.* Low morale, conflict of personalities, lack of preselling of the sales supervisor concept, poor rapport with the home office, tensions within a sales division the candidate may be assigned to —all these may deter him from taking on the responsibilities of sales supervisor.

There are many other reasons why you may not wish to become a sales supervisor. But these six prevail today; they will probably prevail less in the future because management will deal with them more intelligently. You'll want to consider them before accepting promotion to sales supervisor.

Third principle: Be sure you can shift your focus.

A sales supervisor recently recruited from the ranks can't always play the role he needs to play. He may be apologetic in his dealings with his former peers. He may hesitate to demonstrate ways they can improve and grow. He may be embarrassed to point out salesmen's weaknesses and ways of converting them to strengths. His loyalty may remain with the salesmen—he may be oversympathetic to them.

Is there any easy way to determine whether he'll shift focus? No. But one of the surest guides is past actions.

If you have a record for correcting conditions tactfully, if you're constructive in your criticism with due deference to the feelings of others, if you're known for adhering to your convictions without stubbornness—there's basis for some sound predictions. For you're evidently a man of character. This ability to shift focus will play a greater part in your success because of rapidly changing conditions of marketing in the next few years.

Fourth principle: Look to your abilities as a communicator.

The sales supervisor of the immediate future will be a better listener, speaker, reader, and writer than he is today. Let's be arbitrary and suggest definite levels of skills for you to meet.

1. *As a listener* you'll have a longer auditory span, the result of training. You'll have a better memory. Moreover, you'll be adept in the use of the nondirective type of interview. Here you'll listen much more than talk, and you'll be trained to "listen" for tensions and indicators below the surface. You'll be more competent in semantics and its practical application, particularly in evaluating the use of your salesmen's words and their implications.

2. *As a speaker* you'll have greater competence in oral reading, telephone technique, dictation of letters, memos, etc., presiding at meetings, leading discussions and brainstorming sessions, participating in programs of your professional marketing organizations, platform presentation, training your salesmen to be better speakers and listeners.

3. *As a reader* you'll be efficient in skimming or speed-

reading (at least 350 words a minute), in analytical reading, in interpreting figures, graphs, and charts. Moreover, you'll be a man of taste in the selection of reading materials, will keep abreast of marketing, supervision, sales management. Further, you'll read to bear your share of cultural responsibility, will know how to develop good reading habits among your salesmen.

4. *As a writer* you'll practice clarity. Your sentences will be short, your words simple. Your letters, reports, memos, and bulletins will bear the impress of common sense and graciousness. Every piece you write will be motivated by a sense of public relations.

Fifth principle: You'll need to stimulate your superiors as well as your salesmen.

The sales supervisor of the future will be a more vital link between the field force and the home office. You'll know your salesmen and will relay this knowledge to the home office. You'll conceive of salesmanship as a profession, as one facet of a larger complex, marketing.

Your constructive thinking will stimulate your superiors. Your flow of suggestions from the field will egg your management on. You'll keep your management alerted to competitive activity. In your periodic appraisals of your salesmen and their needs, you'll stress the impact of good company organization and administration on their morale.

Sixth principle: Be an eager learner.

In the future the sales supervisor will take part in training or "personal progress programs" to a greater extent than he does today. You'll meet with your colleagues periodically for stimulation and study. You'll attend even more courses offered outside the company than today.

In group learning you'll work well with your peers, share

ideas—profitably developed in your division—with your colleagues. You'll increase your competence in the discussion of case studies. You'll be even more studious than you are today. You'll be dedicated particularly to innovations in your supervisory techniques.

Seventh principle: Be a delegator.

The future sales supervisor will be better prepared to get more production out of his men. You'll be expert in the administration of performance reviews and appraisals. You'll give to each of your salesmen a little more to do than they can comfortably get done. You'll teach them greater efficiency in analyzing their territories and accounts, in streamlining their presentations, in presenting ideas and marketing aids to customers. You'll assign increasingly important accounts to younger salesmen. Your chief goal will be to develop men. Because of your wisdom in delegating increased responsibility, your men will actually promote you faster.

In the climate of confidence you'll create, you'll assume the attitude that your men can't make any mistakes that can't be corrected. You'll encourage your men to make mistakes as learning devices, so long as they don't repeat them. In this way you'll engender an eagerness in them to reach out. As Dr. Saul Gellerman says, "He'll promote the right to be wrong."

Eighth principle: Be a robust candidate.

The sales supervisor of the future will be able to work harder—with fewer breakdowns than his counterpart experiences today. He'll be more mature emotionally. He won't need to bawl out or "ream out" his salesmen. His understanding of himself and his salesmen will make him wiser. He'll expend less energy on frustrations, more on accomplishments. He'll understand human motivation better. He'll use leadership rather than fear or repression to stimulate his men. The whole change of emphasis will cause less wear and tear on his mind and solar plexus. He'll be a healthier sales supervisor in body, mind, and spirit, and morale in his division will be high.

You see how strong and mature you'll need to be to qualify.

Ninth principle: Develop presence.

Napoleon said that the Duke of Wellington's presence on the battlefield was worth 10 battalions. All of us occasionally meet the individual whose mere presence raises morale. The sales supervisor of the future will be more aware of the value of developing a "presence." He'll realize, as Walt Whitman did, that there's more to a man than is found between his boots and his hat. He'll strive to develop the quality of presence in himself and his salesmen.

Tenth principle: Promote from within the organization, where you'll become a policy maker.

This is based on the realization that everyone has a vast, untouched potential, that in every sizable sales force there's a wealth of potential sales supervisors of high caliber. They must be identified by objective methods. In the near future, sales supervisors will be developed from within the company by more carefully planned programs.

Wisely, you'll probably not set an age limit. Two of the best sales supervisors selected a year ago by a large company were twenty-nine and fifty-nine years old, respectively. The former had been with the company four years; the latter, thirty-one years. The latter is one of the youngest-minded, most adaptable, most receptive of all the supervisors. His promotion did a lot for the morale of the older salesmen. Age will be defined more functionally, rather than chronologically, in the future than it is today. When you promote from within you give every ambitious salesman added incentive to work hard. You select men who know the company and its policies. You build loyalty to company. The only time this principle should not be applied is when your personnel does not meet the objective standards you set for your sales supervisors. If this should be the case, your company has probably failed to select competent salesmen in the first place—or has neglected to train them for the future.

A check list to uncover sales supervisors' problems

Their answers will help you to understand what kind of leadership they need, what types of training programs would be the most helpful to them.

Below are 45 items. Before each item is a blank line. After reading through the list of items, write 1 before the 15 items that you believe to be the most urgent in your division, 2 before the 15 of secondary importance, 3 before the 15 least important.

_____1. Giving a formal appraisal to salesmen
_____2. Making suggestions to my division manager
_____3. Scheduling my time so as to give each of my salesmen enough attention
_____4. Helping a salesman with his family problems
_____5. Maintaining communication with home office or outside the division
_____6. Finding enough time to improve myself
_____7. Keeping my wife happy
_____8. Living within my salary
_____9. Understanding company policy—in certain respects

__10. Doing my job as I understand it and think it should be done

__11. Spending enough time with my family

__12. Feeling that I am growing in the dispatch of my responsibilities as supervisor

__13. Traveling too much

__14. Having the confidence of my boss

__15. Feeling that I am adequately paid

__16. Living in the part of the country where I am stationed

__17. Developing my salesmen's confidence in me

__18. Taking part in community responsibilities

__19. Following a course of reading

__20. Writing personal notes and letters

__21. Developing better dealer relations

__22. Keeping happy

__23. Having someone to share my quandaries

__24. Helping my salesmen to analyze their territories

__25. Training my salesmen methodically

__26. Keeping in good physical shape

__27. Interpreting company policy to my boss

__28. Speaking with salesmen constructively about their shortcomings

__29. Being a good model for my salesmen

__30. Understanding and interpreting our advertising policies

__31. Supervising and upgrading the older salesmen under my supervision

__32. Training my salesmen in making better presentations

__33. Developing a system of checking on my salesmen's work habits

__34. Helping my salesmen simplify their paper work

___35. Making new salesmen feel that they are part of the team

___36. Using a report form to give each salesman on each of my visits with him—to let him know how he has progressed since my last visit with him

___37. Developing greater morale in my division

___38. Meeting my cultural responsibilities

___39. Helping salesmen to get in to see important accounts

___40. Keeping myself from getting discouraged or depressed

___41. Developing closer relations with salesmen of other divisions of the company

___42. Making constructive suggestions to the home office

___43. Setting my goals for heavier responsibility within the company

___44. Following through on the ideas given at training or sales meetings

___45. Recommending that poor salesmen be separated

Still interested in the promotion? If you are, you'll appreciate what Confucius has to say.

Confucius had the secret

When Confucius—the great lawgiver of China—retired from the Court of Peking, he returned to the village of his youth. He was old and tired after a long, distinguished career. He wanted to spend the sunset years in the simple life.

It was his wont to go each day and sit in the village square. How good the warm sun felt as he sat against the wall! He could look at the passing scene or doze—just as he chose.

Now it came to pass in the spring of the year that the

young mandarins of the village returned from their studies. They were proud and boastful of their intellectuality. And they looked down their noses at Confucius, "that old has-been." Daily the young fellows would seek out Confucius in the village square. They would try to get him in a box with their learning. And of course he would always best them.

One day the ringleader caught a little bird. He said to his companions, "Now, I've got Confucius where I want him! I'll say to him, 'O! Master. Prove thy wisdom. Between my palms is a little bird. Tell me, O Wise One, is it alive or is it dead?' "

"If he says, 'Dead,' I'll open my palms and the little bird will fly away. But if he says, 'Alive,' I'll smother it and show him it's dead. How can we lose?"

They heartily agreed that now they had old Confucius where they wanted him. And so they hurried to the village square. They made a semicircle before him. And their leader spoke, "O Master, we have caught a little bird. I hold it between my palms. Tell us, O Wise One, is it alive or is it dead?"

Confucius rubbed his back against the wall, blinked at the sun, and said, "The answer, my son, is in your own hands!"

Index